A Guide to Financial Decisions

PLANNING FOR THE END OF LIFE

CA Chartered Accountants of Canada

Published by the Canadian Institute of Chartered Accountants

Materials adapted with permission from:
- The American Institute of Certified Public Accountants, Inc. ©2009
- The Michigan Association of Certified Public Accountants and the Hospice of Michigan ©2009.

Library and Archives Canada Cataloguing in Publication

    A guide to financial decisions : planning for the end of life.

ISBN 978-1-55385-537-8

    1. Older people--Canada--Finance, Personal. 2. Estate planning--Canada.   I. Canadian Institute of Chartered Accountants

HG179.G8554 2012   332.0240084'60971   C2010-907402-5

Copyright © 2012
The Canadian Institute of Chartered Accountants
277 Wellington Street West
Toronto ON M5V 3H2

Printed and bound in Canada

A GUIDE TO

FINANCIAL DECISIONS

IMPLEMENTING AN END-OF-LIFE PLAN

The material contained in this booklet is designed to introduce some fundamental topics related to managing the period leading up to the end of life. It is important to plan ahead because families often struggle with financial matters during an extended illness. Doing so ensures family members can address issues quickly and efficiently. This booklet provides the necessary background when working with a competent advisor, and explains the most important questions you should ask. It provides easy-to-understand definitions of key terms and information for persons facing extended illness, and for the families of those who are ill or recently deceased. There is also a helpful list of resources which includes Website addresses for accessing information on the Internet and a glossary of important terms. After you read this *Guide*, the best advice we can offer is to consult with a competent advisor, such as a Chartered Accountant or lawyer, where applicable, for assistance in addressing these challenging financial issues.

Disclaimer: This *Guide* is intended as a basic resource guide for end-of-life issues. This *Guide* should not be construed as providing financial or legal advice and it is not intended to replace the advice and the expertise of a qualified professional in the accounting, legal, or financial planning professions. Working with a qualified professional is strongly recommended. The points covered herein are merely introductory, and therefore the content of this *Guide* should not be presumed to be exhaustive. Applicable tax rules, laws and regulations change frequently and may have changed since the preparation of this *Guide*. The material in this *Guide* should be verified against the specific laws within your province or territory.

PERSONAL REFLECTIONS
OF AN ElderCare CA

My mother died at the age of 76. She suffered very little in her final days. People often say "it's a blessing" when death comes quickly and peacefully, and the person has lived a full life and achieved a good age.

Our family situation was unique because our father died in 1965, when my two sisters and I were still very young. Our mother, who was only 42, was faced with the task of raising her three children alone in a time when community support systems for single parent families did not exist.

However, our extended family and our church family provided the support we needed to work our way through the challenges, particularly in the early years. In addition to suddenly becoming a single parent, my mother was faced with the daunting task of maintaining the household and the finances on her own.

Fortunately, my mother was able to sell the family business, thereby securing our financial future. This allowed her to concentrate on bringing emotional stability into the home and help her children to grow and develop. I will always be grateful for the success of my father's business as it still provided financial stability to our family through my mother's lifetime.

My first encounter with a Chartered Accountant was when our "family CA" came to our home to assist my mother in finalizing the business sale transaction. Our CA guided my mother through this new experience of managing financial resources and she was grateful for the interest and care he displayed. I later consulted with this same family CA when I was contemplating my own career path.

In my mother's later years I became involved in managing her financial affairs when the responsibility became a burden for her. Since I was in Alberta and she was in Saskatchewan, I arranged to receive documentation of all her financial affairs, so that I could manage her bank account and investments. When I started this process in the early 1990s, I didn't realize that I was already practising Elder-Care. Meanwhile, my sister monitored our mother's health and home care issues. My two sisters and I regularly discussed her health and home care issues. As our mother became frail, our involvement in her total care increased.

After our mother's passing, the family dealt with the immediate funeral plans, and then sorted out her financial assets and personal possessions. My financial records were able to provide a clear picture, allowing for ease of allocation. It was the culmination of a successful ElderCare engagement, heavy on the emotion since it was my own family.

In my own accounting practice, I have provided similar ElderCare services for clients. The personal experience in caring for my mother's affairs led me to provide these services within my practice. I joined the CICA/AICPA ElderCare Task Force in 1997, not knowing exactly what to expect. I knew I wanted to hone my own skills in this new service area and thought that my personal experience would enable me to make a useful contribution to the Task Force.

Michael Epp, CA
Member, CICA PrimePlus Task Force
Partner, Hawkings Epp Dumont

ACKNOWLEDGEMENTS

The Canadian Institute of Chartered Accountants (CICA) wishes to acknowledge the contributions and assistance of many organizations in the completion of this resource *guide*. This book is the result of a vision brought to the American Institute of Certified Public Accountants (AICPA) by Hospice of Michigan and the Michigan Association of Certified Public Accountants and adapted by the CICA for Canadian purposes.

THE MICHIGAN ASSOCIATION OF CERTIFIED PUBLIC ACCOUNTANTS (MACPA)

Recognizing there was no resource available to those in the end of life, the MACPA formed a task force specifically to address this issue and develop the resource guide *Financial Affairs: At the End of Life*. In partnership with Hospice of Michigan, MACPA members spent hours discussing, diagramming and creating this product to ensure its success with patients and the community at large. Their unwavering support and generous donation of time and talent have been valuable gifts.

HOSPICE OF MICHIGAN

We appreciate the staff of Hospice of Michigan and their work with patients and their families at an extremely difficult and vulnerable time. Every day they see the consequences of financial turmoil on persons with life-limiting illness, and the suffering of families that lasts far beyond the death of their loved one when financial planning was neglected. The staff's desire to provide patients with practical financial information and their commitment in reviewing and contributing to the *Guide* reflects their dedication to their profession and patients.

THE AMERICAN INSTITUTE OF CERTIFIED PUBLIC ACCOUNTANTS' (AICPA'S) PERSONAL FINANCIAL PLANNING EXECUTIVE COMMITTEE

The volunteer members of this committee continue to provide leadership and guidance on financial planning initiatives. Their support and input for this *Guide* have been instrumental in its completion and distribution.

THE PrimePlus/ElderCare TASK FORCE

This joint task force of the Canadian Institute of Chartered Accountants (CICA) and the American Institute of Certified Public Accountants (AICPA) provided both content and reviews for the *Guide*. We appreciate their support and passion for meeting the needs of a maturing population.

Portions of this Guide contain material reprinted with permission from The American Institute of Certified Public Accountants and Michigan Hospice Association.

THE CANADIAN PRIMEPLUS TASK FORCE

David Braumberger CA, Michael Epp CA, William Hyde CA and Kelly Lohn CA provided the Canadian content for the *Guide*. Their dedication to this project has been crucial to the completion of the *Guide* for Canadian users.

TABLE OF CONTENTS

INTRODUCTION

Throughout your life, you have likely set goals for yourself both financially and personally. Chances are, the goals that have been most successfully fulfilled are the ones you planned for. Planning helps to focus on what's important to you, identifies the steps that need to be accomplished to get there, provides a framework for keeping you on track and gives you the opportunity to make adjustments when needed. Planning for one's end of life can be uncomfortable and it is easy to deny the inevitable by just not thinking or talking about it. However, like most things in life, if you don't plan for it, there will be no plan. This *Guide* has been developed to help you think about your end of life plan and how that plan can help with your own peace of mind and quality of life. This *Guide* also helps you consider your family members and how you can make the transition of your passing easier for them. After reading this *Guide* and reflecting on the topics that are discussed here, contact your Chartered Accountant who can help you develop a plan that is created especially for you and your family.

CHAPTER 1

PLANNING FOR YOURSELF

To help you in your planning, it is a good idea to seek the help of a Chartered Accountant, lawyer, financial planner or insurance agent who has specific knowledge and experience in the topics for which you are requesting advice. Chartered Accountants can help individuals with a variety of financial issues, including tax assistance, financial planning, management consulting and valuation services for businesses. Many Chartered Accountants also have expertise in providing services to elderly clients and their families, including designing, implementing and monitoring financial strategies for maturing individuals and families to assist them in maintaining and enjoying their personal independence.

1.1 HEALTH, MEDICAL AND FINANCIAL DECISION-MAKING

During an illness, it can be difficult or impossible to communicate your wishes about what kinds of health-care decisions you would like made on your behalf. Advance care planning enables you to state your wishes before you become ill. Relevant documents discussed in this section should be updated at least every five years. Talk to your legal advisor if something major happens.

If you do not plan ahead for a possible mental incapacity, the court will decide who is to handle affairs relating to your property, including paying your bills and maintaining or selling any of your property such as your house or car. Health care decisions can usually be made by your next of kin depending on the applicable substitute health care consent legislation. The court process, however, can be time consuming and costly with no guarantee of your desired result. Time limits for serving the documents and who needs to be served are set out in the legislation. Your legal advisor can provide specific guidance.

1.1.1 LIVING WILL/ADVANCE DIRECTIVE

A living will expresses the wishes and desires of a patient when death is imminent or further treatment would be of no real benefit. Typically, advance directives may include statements to the effect that, in the event of a coma or impending death, no unusual means are to be used to resuscitate or prolong life. These directives may be so specific as to specifically indicate which life support equipment is not to be used and that nourishment and liquids are to be withheld. There may also be cases when the living will directs the doctors to use all available means to prolong life, even if the ill person will never regain consciousness or will be permanently impaired as a result of the treatment. Provincial legislation governs the making of living wills and advance directives in those jurisdictions that have implemented applicable legislation. Where there is no applicable legislation, provincial legislation dictates whether or not living wills and advance directives are permissible. In jurisdictions that have not legislated advance directives or living wills, a mentally capable person can express their wishes in writing. A person making a living will should consult their doctor to understand the issues involved. Living wills should be prepared by a lawyer who is competent in such matters and familiar with the laws of the applicable jurisdiction. Copies of the living will should be provided to the patient's primary doctor, family members and their Chartered Accountant.

1.1.2 POWERS OF ATTORNEY FOR PERSONAL CARE/ HEALTH CARE PROXY

A power of attorney for personal care or health care proxy addresses much broader health care issues. These powers of attorney may be limited or unlimited and grant someone the authority to make medical decisions on behalf of the principal and to respond to changing health and medical needs as they occur. In situations where an advance directive regarding health care decisions has not been made or a guardian has not been appointed by the court, family members, depending on their relationship to the patient, may be authorized by legislation to act on behalf of the patient.

If you have private health insurance, be sure to give information regarding the insurer as well as all relevant identification numbers to your next of kin or substitute health care decision-maker. Even if you are in a nursing home, this information will be required for extended benefits, such as a semi-private or private room if you are unexpectedly hospitalized.

1.1.3 POWER OF ATTORNEY FOR PROPERTY

A power of attorney for property (a mandate in anticipation of incapacity in Québec) is a document in which one person grants another person the power to act or deal with their property on their behalf. The relationship is one of agency, meaning that the title to the property, such as a bank account or property deed, remains in the name of the person granting the power of attorney. In legislation across the provinces and territories this person is the "donor", except in Ontario and Saskatchewan (the "grantor") and in Quebec (the "mandator"). For the purposes of this discussion, the person granting the power of attorney is the "principal". The person acting on behalf of the principal is the "attorney", except in New Brunswick (the "donee") and Quebec (the "mandatary"). For the purpose of this discussion, this person will be the "agent". In Québec, a mandate in anticipation of incapacity must be homologated by the court in order to become effective. Homologation is required to verify that the mandator is incompetent and to ensure the existence of the mandate and that it is valid.

Rights granted to the agent can be specific (for example, acting for the principal to pay the bills during a hospital stay) or general, which gives the agent the power to basically do anything that the principal can legally do, subject to prescribed exceptions.

A specific power of attorney that is granted to a person is usually a non-revocable power of attorney, i.e., the power ceases when the task provided by the power of attorney is completed.

A general power of attorney is usually revocable and remains effective until the principal revokes the power of attorney, dies, or becomes mentally incapable. A power of attorney can continue in the event of the principal's mental incapacity, if certain conditions are met. The principal must be mentally competent to revoke a power of attorney.

A continuing or enduring power of attorney will contain a prescribed clause stating that the power will continue during the incapacity of the principal. Generally a continuing or enduring power of attorney becomes effective at the time that it is signed but it does not mean that the principal cannot deal with their own property. Often, the principal will choose to deal with their own property while mentally capable. It is recommended that an executed continuing or enduring power of attorney be left with a trusted third party with instructions regarding determining whether or not the principal is mentally incapable.

Some jurisdictions provide that the principal may choose whether or not the power of attorney comes into effect at the time of execution or on some future date or contingent event, such as mental incapacity. This is known as a springing power of attorney. The governing legislation generally provides a procedure for determining when the contingent event has occurred.

All powers of attorney are governed by the applicable provincial or territorial legislation. Formalities are required, such as number of witnesses, minimum age of the principal and agent, and use of a prescribed form and/or language to make a power of attorney. You should consult a lawyer skilled in such matters when making a power of attorney or reviewing an existing power of attorney regarding whether it still meets your needs.

Banks often require that their own power of attorney document be completed even if a principal has given an agent authority to write cheques and make deposits and withdrawals on their behalf. It is best to inquire if your bank will recognize a power of attorney or will require its own form.

1.1.4 CHOOSING SOMEONE TO MAKE DECISIONS FOR YOU

Persons chosen as substitute decision-makers (agents) should be carefully considered for their trustworthiness, reliability, compatibility with other interested parties, willingness to act and ability to deal with professionals such as Chartered Accountants, lawyers and health care providers to make appropriate decisions in the other person's best interests. An alternate agent should also be considered in case a person's first choice cannot act. At times, multiple agents may also be desirable. Provincial legislation will generally specify how the agents are to act, unless otherwise stated by the principal in the document.

If no enduring power of attorney exists and a person is no longer competent to execute such a document, a friend or family member may choose to apply to court to become guardian or similar representative of the principal's property. The Public

Trustee, Public Guardian and Trustee or similar public office, depending on the jurisdiction, may also apply to court to manage a person's affairs. In either of these cases, there is no guarantee that the guardian appointed by the court would be the principal's choice. To avoid this outcome, everyone should have a power of attorney.

> Advance directives take the "crisis mode" out of decision-making

1.1.5 DO NOT RESUSCITATE (DNR)

A do not resuscitate (DNR) order instructs medical personnel not to perform lifesaving cardiopulmonary resuscitation (CPR) or other procedures to restart the heart or breathing once they have ceased. The physician can write an order on a patient's health record with regard to a living will or advance directive or if, in the physician's judgment, resuscitating the patient would be futile or not beneficial. Be certain that your physician and the person named as your health care proxy are aware of a DNR order if you have one. In this situation, a physician should communicate with the patient, family and hospice staff to establish a treatment plan.

1.2 PLANNING TO MEET FINANCIAL NEEDS

Many families experience a significant change in their financial situation as a result of a loved one's illness or death. Meeting short-term and long-term expenses and commitments and achieving a sense of security may become problematic.

The introduction of a terminal illness or death into a family or household can cause many types of changes. Worries about medical expenses, loss of income and an uncertain future can combine to weigh heavily on you and your family. You may find you:
- charge purchases you don't really need
- make only the minimum down payments on your credit card
- take cash advances on credit cards
- borrow more and more money from family and friends
- use your cash reserves to pay bills
- receive new bills before old ones are paid
- reach or exceed your credit limit.

This section discusses the best way to access financial resources and manage your affairs in these circumstances. Some options may be more beneficial than others and the impact on the family's financial situation should be considered carefully.

1.2.1 DISABILITY INSURANCE

Disability insurance coverage is designed to pay your expenses while you are disabled and cannot work. If you are employed you may be covered through your benefits coverage. You have to meet a strict definition of disability to qualify for benefits from government programs (e.g., CPP/QPP) and, therefore, should not rely on them as your only source of income in the event you become disabled. Instead, find out if you have group disability insurance through your employer. It may be paid for by the company, or you may pay part of the premium. If disability coverage is not available at work or if you are self-employed, you should consider purchasing an individual policy from a private insurer. Most policies pay between 50 and 70% of your gross income for anywhere from a couple of months to age 65. The premium may vary depending on the waiting period.

> **Do you have any disability insurance?**
>
> **Are you owed benefits?**

Employment Insurance also offers sick leave benefits to insured employees. If you are self-employed, you may wish to consider signing up with the Employment Insurance Commission for coverage of sickness benefits and compassionate care benefits. Compassionate care benefits provide insured workers the ability to take time off work to care for a gravely ill relative who is at significant risk of dying. There is a waiting period prior to making a claim for either sickness benefits or compassionate care benefits and the benefits are provided only for a specific number of weeks. For further information, contact Service Canada at **www.servicecanada.gc.ca**.

1.2.2 CANADA PENSION PLAN DISABILITY BENEFITS

Canada Pension Plan (CPP) disability benefits provide a monthly taxable benefit to contributors who are disabled. In order to be eligible for these benefits you must be under 65 years of age, have stopped working because of your severe and prolonged disability, and have paid into CPP for at least four of the past six years or, if you have paid into CPP for at least 25 years, you must have made contributions to the plan in three of the past six years. A few exceptions to these conditions are possibly available if the applicant stayed at home and raised children, applied too late for the

CPP disability benefit, separated or divorced, lived and worked in another country or was physically or mentally unable to apply.

The benefit amount a person receives includes a base benefit plus an amount based on how much one has contributed to the CPP during one's working career. The maximum disability benefit is increased annually according to the cost of living index.

Applications can be made online or by contacting Canada Pension Plan for an application package, which includes a questionnaire, application and medical report, to be completed and forwarded to your local Service Canada office. Applications are generally processed within 120 days. Applicants who are terminally ill receive priority and their applications are generally reviewed within 48 hours of receipt of the application. See **www.hrsdc.gc.ca/cgi-bin/search/eforms/index.cgi? app=profile&form=isp1151&lang=eng**

1.2.3 REGISTERED DISABILITY SAVINGS PLANS

A Registered Disability Savings Plan (RDSP) provides taxpayers with the opportunity to contribute up to a prescribed maximum of $200,000 for a beneficiary, up to age 59, who qualifies for the disability tax credit. Although contributions to an RDSP are not tax deductible, earnings within the RDSP are not taxable. For beneficiaries who are 49 years of age or younger in a tax year, the Canada Disability Savings Grant and Canada Disability Savings Bond may increase the amount of the RDSP. This increase requires that families meet an income test. Note that withdrawals from a RDSP that exceed contributions are taxable.

Recent changes permit a beneficiary with a shortened life expectancy to withdraw taxable amounts up to $10,000 per year from their RDSP without having to repay amounts received from Canada Disability Savings Bonds and Canada Disability Savings Grants deposited in their RDSP within the last 10 years. A medical doctor must certify in writing that, in their opinion, the beneficiary has a maximum life expectancy of up to five years. The beneficiary must elect on the prescribed form and submit it, along with the medical certificate, to their RDSP issuer. The RDSP issuer will notify the Minister of Human Resource and Skills Development Canada, making the plan a Specified Plan. Special contribution and withdrawal rules apply while the RDSP is a Specified Plan.

1.2.4 VETERAN AFFAIRS CANADA

Veteran Affairs Canada administers a wide array of benefits under the New Veterans Charter for qualified veterans, Canadian Forces members, RCMP members (including discharged members), certain civilians and their families. Some of the services offered under the New Veterans Charter include financial benefits, group health insurance, lump sum disability amounts, survivor benefits and rehabilitation. A Services and Benefits Guide can be downloaded at **www.vac-acc.gc.ca**.

Benefits are available for veterans

The *Enhanced New Veterans Charter Act* received Royal Assent on March 24, 2011 and is to be proclaimed into force. The *Act* will broaden the scope of the eligibility of seriously injured veterans for monthly allowances for life. An additional monthly supplement will be available for injured or ill veterans who cannot return to suitable work. New payment options will be available for those receiving a disability award.

Information about disability pensions can be found in the section on Disability Pensions at the Veteran Affairs Canada Website at **www.vac-acc.gc.ca** or by calling 1-866-522-2122.

Veterans may be eligible for home care. See the Veteran Independence Program at **www.vac-acc.gc.ca** or by calling 1-866-522-2122.

Long-term or chronic care is available to qualified war Veterans and certain civilians. The Support for Operational Stress Network is available through Operational Stress Injury clinics if medically referred by a VAC medical officer.

The Operational Stress Injury Social Support (OSISS) program has established a Peer Support Network to help Canadian Forces members, Veterans and their families deal with OSI. A Peer Support Coordinator can be contacted at 1-800-883-6094 or at **www.osiss.ca**.

Mental Health brochures can also be downloaded by at **www.vac-acc.gc.ca** or by calling 1-866-522-2122.

1.2.5 LONG-TERM CARE INSURANCE

Long-term care (LTC) insurance is purchased when you are healthy and is designed to pay a daily benefit if you require home care or are admitted to a long-term care facility. To receive a benefit, a doctor must certify that you require extended health care because of injury, sickness, cognitive impairment, or the inability to perform two or more of the daily activities of living (such as bathing, dressing, toileting, eating, walking, transferring, bladder control, or taking medication.)

There are a number of options when choosing LTC insurance. LTC Insurance Benefits can cover just facility care, or both home care and facility care. You can purchase any amount of coverage subject to a minimum and maximum daily amount. You may also select the length of time you wish to wait prior to receiving benefits (waiting period) and the length of time you wish to receive benefits once you qualify.

An individual should consider purchasing long-term care insurance if they have significant assets that they wish to protect, they expect they will be paying for the care they require and they wish to maintain their independence. The cost of premiums over 10 years could be less than one year of nursing home costs. The Council on Aging of Ottawa has produced a guide, *Long Term Care Insurance in Canada: What is it and do I need it?*, which can be accessed from their online library holdings at **www.coaottawa.ca**.

A variation of long-term care insurance is Critical Care or critical illness insurance, whereby the insurer is contracted to make a lump-sum cash payment if the policyholder is diagnosed with one of the critical illnesses listed in the policy. Cover-

> Check that Alzheimer's disease and other forms of dementia are covered when considering long-term care insurance

age may be denied to applicants who have previously had or have an illness such as AIDS or cancer, or an underlying condition such as insulin-dependent diabetes.

The Canadian Association of Retired Persons (CARP) provides information on different insurance plans including long-term care insurance and critical illness insurance. For more information see **www.carp.ca**.

1.2.6 RETIREMENT ACCOUNTS AND PENSIONS

There are many different kinds of retirement accounts and pensions. As part of the process of gathering information and planning for the future, it is a good idea to get a sense of how many and which kind you have. Review your investments from financial and similar institutions. Some are provided by an employer, so it is important to remember both current and past employers, including the military, when gathering documents on these accounts. Determine whether you can name a beneficiary for your plan's assets or review your earlier beneficiary choice to make it reflect your current wishes. You may find answers to many questions by reviewing the benefits handbook of your current employer. Once you create a list of the ones you have, you can begin to consider some key questions. For example:

- What benefits are available in the event of disability, retirement or death?
- Have you chosen a beneficiary for each account?
- Does that choice need to be updated?
- How do your choices fit into your overall estate plan?

83.9% of all public sector employees participate in a Registered Pension Plan (RPP)

Pension Plans in Canada Survey at January 1, 2008: Statistics Canada, *The Daily*, Monday June 8, 2009

Approximately 25% of all private sector employees participate in a Registered Pension Plan (RPP)

Pension Plans in Canada Survey at January 1, 2008: Statistics Canada, *The Daily*, Monday June 8, 2009

Your Chartered Accountant can help you answer these and other questions.

A union in a specific industry where it is common for workers to have many employers, such as in the construction industry, may have information about pension entitlements with respect to multi-employer pension plans, specified multi-employer plans or similar plans.

Also determine whether you have an existing retirement account from a former employer. If you withdrew your plan's assets when you left a job or had the plan's assets transferred to another type of retirement plan, no additional steps are necessary. There still may be a deferred pension plan with a former employer.

Note: You may need to search for these benefits. Review prior year tax returns (as far back as possible) and contact prior employers. Be aware that some of the companies where you worked could have since been absorbed by another business or gone bankrupt.

The first important step is to identify all of your possible accounts and resources, including accounts from which you are currently receiving payments. Make sure you are receiving, or will receive, all the retirement benefits you are entitled to.

1.2.7 CANADA PENSION PLAN/ QUEBEC PENSION PLAN

Canada Pension Plan (CPP)/Quebec Pension Plan (QPP) benefits are available to eligible Canadians who have made contributions during their working life. Retirement payments are payable at age 65 depending on the number of years you contributed and the prescribed maximum amount. You can begin receiving retirement benefits as early as 60 years old at a reduced amount or you can continue to work and postpone receiving benefits until you are 70 years old at which time you will receive a higher amount. You can ask Services Canada for a Contribution of Earnings. If you live in Quebec, you can contact Régie des rentes du Québec.

1.2.8 OLD AGE SECURITY

The Old Age Security (OAS) is a monthly benefit available for most Canadians 65 years of age or older, who have been resident in Canada for a minimum of 10 years after reaching the age of 18. The maximum monthly benefit is indexed quarterly per year to reflect adjustments to the consumer price index. Pensioners with individual net income in excess of an annual income threshold must repay part or all of the maximum OAS pension. For current average and monthly amounts as well as income thresholds, see **www.servicecanada.gc.ca/eng/isp/oas/ oasrates.shtml**

Approximately 5.9 million Canadian workers have a membership in an employer pension plan

Statistics Canada: *The Daily*, March 16, 2010

What employee benefits do you have available for death or disability?

Approximately 1.65 million people who are 45 years of age or older help a parent or parent-in-law who has a physical disability or long-term health issue

Statistics Canada: *The Daily*, January 26, 2010

1.2.9 GUARANTEED INCOME SUPPLEMENT

The Guaranteed Income Supplement (GIS) provides additional money on top of the Old Age Security Pension to low income seniors living in Canada. To receive the annual GIS you must be receiving the OAS pension. The GIS is based on your annual income or the combined annual income of you and your spouse (or common law partner). Since annual incomes change from year to year, the GIS, like the OAS, must be renewed each year. This is done automatically by filing your personal tax return by April 30th. If a tax return is not filed, then a renewal application must be forwarded to Service Canada. The GIS is subject to a low income test and stops being payable if the maximum income threshold has been exceeded. See **www.servicecanada.gc.ca/eng/isp/oas/oasrates.shtml**.

Effective July 1, 2011, low-income seniors will receive an additional benefit to their Old Age Security (OAS) and Guaranteed Income Supplement (GIS) benefits. Single seniors with little or no annual income, other than their OAS and GIS benefits, can receive up to $600 per year. Senior couples with little or no income, other than their OAS and GIS benefits, can receive up to $840 per year.

CPP, OAS and GIS benefits can be paid by direct deposit to your bank account. This is generally done on the third-last banking day each month, except in December when it is deposited on the third-last banking day before Christmas Day. Alternatively, cheques can be mailed directly to the recipient. Both CPP and OAS can be received on a non-resident basis. GIS is only available for Canadian residents. See **www.servicecanada.gc.ca/eng/isp/common/paydates.shtml**

QPP deposits are made on the last working day each month. See **www.rrq.gouv. qc.ca/en/dates_paiement/Pages/dates_paiement_regime_rente.aspx**

Seniors in many provinces and the territories may be entitled to receive benefits under a supplementary income plan if they meet an income test or other conditions.

1.2.10 WITHDRAWING FUNDS FROM A REGISTERED RETIREMENT SAVINGS PLAN

Early withdrawal of funds from a Registered Retirement Savings Plan (RRSP) may appear to be a great source of funds during an emergency, however, early withdrawals will affect the growth potential of the RRSP and the amount withdrawn is subject to withholding tax. The percentage of withholding tax varies depending on the amount withdrawn.

1.2.11 REGISTERED RETIREMENT INCOME FUND

You can transfer your RRSP amount to a Registered Retirement Income Fund (RRIF) when your RRSP matures in order to defer paying taxes on the full amount at that time. Rather than withdrawing the full amount of your RRSP and being subject to tax, you can transfer your RRSP into a Registered Retirement Income Fund (RRIF). Withdrawals begin in the following year. Although you are still subject to tax on amounts received, you are only required to withdraw a minimum prescribed amount per year. This income qualifies for the pension tax credit. A RRIF must be established by the year-end in which an RRSP or RPP annuitant turns 71 years old, at the latest. A prescribed annual minimum must begin to be paid out of the RRIF in the following year.

The 2011 Budget and legislative proposals propose to reduce tax deferral opportunities for Individual Pension Plans (IPPs) by requiring minimum annual withdrawal requirements similar to the minimum withdrawal rules for RRIFs, effective for 2012. Restrictions are also proposed to be applied to contributions with respect to past service.

A defined benefit RPP will be designated as an Individual Pension Plan under the new rules where the plan has a maximum of three members and a minimum of one member is related to a participating employer or the plan is a designated plan where a minimum 50% of the plan members total pension adjustments are owned by connected individuals to the employer or the employees themselves are highly compensated. The plan will be designated an IPP where it would be reasonable to conclude that at least one member's rights exist to avoid the definition.

The Minister has the discretion to waive a plan's status as an IPP where the Minister finds the circumstances appropriate.

1.2.12 TAX-FREE SAVINGS ACCOUNTS

A Tax-Free Savings Account (TFSA) is an investment vehicle created by the Income Tax Act to encourage people to save for big purchase items. While the contributions paid into a TFSA are not tax-deductible the income earned on the savings is not taxable and any amount in a TFSA can be withdrawn at any time without penalty. There is a maximum annual deposit amount which is indexed annually for each Canadian resident who is at least 18 years old and unused contribution room can be carried forward indefinitely. Amounts withdrawn are reinstated the following year in contribution room. Similar to RRSPs and RRIFS, a TFSA account holder is deemed to receive the fair market value of the TFSA immediately before death. Any increase after death in amounts distributed to beneficiaries is taxed in their hands. In some situations this may not apply. For instance, the spouse/common-law partner can, immediately before the death of the TFSA account holder or before the end of the calendar year following the year in which the TFSA account holder dies, designate the amount in a TFSA to be an exempt contribution as a survivor payment to their own TFSA. The contribution must be designated in prescribed form within 30 days of being made. Draft legislation announced in 2010 proposes to expand the definition of "holder (which currently permits the initial holder to designate a survivor to be the initial holder of the TFSA) to permit the successor survivor to designate their own successor survivor and revoke any designations of beneficiary made by the survivor (applicable to 2009 and subsequent taxation years).

1.2.12.1 RRSPs/RRIFs — Anti-Avoidance Rules

The 2011 Federal Budget proposes to introduce anti-avoidance rules for RRSPs/RRIFs that are similar to TFSAs. The provisions address transactions that give an annuitant an advantage, or involve prohibited investments or non-qualified investments.

Transactions that give an annuitant an advantage, such as removing funds from the RRSP/RRIF or that involve a swap transaction that shifts value from an RRSP/RRIF without including the amount in income, will be taxed at 100% of the fair market value of the advantage.

Income earned on a prohibited investment, which includes a debt or investment in a "significant investment" or with which the annuitant does not deal at arm's length, will also be taxed at 100%. A "significant investment" generally includes a debt or investment where the annuitant or a non-arm's length person holds at least 10% of the investment. The fair market value of the prohibited investment is subject to a 50% tax.

Non-qualified investments taxed at 50% of their fair market value. Under certain circumstances this tax may be refundable. "Non-qualified investments" are investments that are not qualified investments as prescribed by the *Income Tax Act* and will be subject to tax at 100% of their fair market value if they are not removed from an RRSP within 90 days of being notified by the Minister of National Revenue.

These proposals are generally applicable to transactions that occur after March 22, 2011 and to income earned on non-qualified or prohibited investments after March 22, 2011.

1.2.13 PENSION SPLITTING PROVISIONS

You and your spouse/common-law partner can reallocate up to one-half of private pension income between you to be eligible to claim the pension credit for the tax year. You must each elect to do so in prescribed form by your filing deadline for the taxation year. This may also be done in certain circumstances when a spouse/common-law partner dies.

1.2.14 U.S. SOCIAL SECURITY BENEFITS

The net inclusion rate of U.S. Social Security Benefits received by Canadian residents and their spouses/common-law partners on or after January 1, 2010 is changed to 50% from 85%, who have continued to receive these benefits since before 1996.

1.2.15 FEDERAL GOVERNMENT INITIATIVES

The federal government recognizes the importance of having a retirement income system in Canada to help seniors live a quality life. Over recent years, the government has:

- increased the age limit when Canadians must stop investing in their Registered Retirement Savings Plans (RRSPs) from 69 years of age to 71 and begin withdrawing a pension under a Registered Retirement Income Fund (RRIF) the following year;
- permitted phased retirement arrangements under defined Registered Pension Plans to allow workers to continue working while receiving a pension;
- introduced the Tax-Free Savings Account to help Canadians save for big ticket purchases without being taxed on the interest earned on their savings; and
- permitted senior couples to split pension income.

Recent changes to CPP/QPP include:

1. removal of the work cessation test in 2012 which will allow workers to retire as young as 60 years of age without any work interruptions;

2. increase incrementally from 2012 to 2014 the number of low-income years that are dropped from the calculation to determine your pension benefit;

3. effective January 1, 2012, require workers under 65 years old who receive a CPP retirement benefit to continue to contribute as well as their employers if they keep working;

4. effective January 1, 2012, permit workers 65 to 70 who receive a CPP retirement benefit as of January 1, 2012 to contribute voluntarily and, if so, their employers will be required to contribute;

5. the early pension reduction for each month for pensioners who take their pension prior to age 65 and as early as age 60 will gradually be increased over five years between 2012 and 2016; and

6. the late pension augmentation for each month for pensioners who take their pension after turning 65 up to age 70 will gradually be increased over three years between 2011 and 2013.

The federal government is continuing the process of improving the federal public pension plan system by meeting with provincial and territorial finance ministers. For further developments, consult your advisor on how potential changes to the Canada Pension Plan may affect you in the future.

1.3 PLANNING YOUR LIVING ARRANGEMENTS

Don't make any rash, quick decisions.

For homeowners, options for reducing expenses or tapping equity include:

- Stay at home and rent out rooms. This provides income. Avoid making emotional decisions.
- Rent out your residence and move to a relative's home or apartment. This option will also provide income, but the tax advantages and disadvantages should be weighed appropriately. It may affect your principle residence exemption. The *Income Tax Act* exempts the capital gain from tax on your home during the years that you and your family or a family member lives in your home. You can only designate one principal residence in a year. It is possible to rent out your home without affecting your principal residence exemption if you file an election for each year you rent to a maximum of four years. Professional advice is recommended.
- Consider selling the home if it is declining in value or the neighborhood is unsafe.
- Consider creating a trust to hold your principal residence.
- Obtain a reverse equity mortgage, but be aware that the upfront costs can be very high.
- Determine if you can defer your property taxes.

> Aging at home can provide dignity and independence, but it must be safe and practical

1.3.1 REVERSE MORTGAGES

A reverse mortgage allows homeowners who are 60 years of age and older to borrow money against the equity in their home for any purpose, such as to pay health care costs or to augment their retirement income. The advantages of a reverse mortgage are:

- You can enjoy some of the equity you have built up in your home over the years and still live in your home;
- There is no tax payable on the money you are borrowing; and
- The income does not affect government income supplement plans such as Old Age Security and Guaranteed Income Supplement.

You may have heard the term "CHIP loan", which is the Canadian Home Income Plan; this is a private company that offers reverse mortgages in Canada. Some financial institutions also offer reverse mortgages. The disadvantages of a reverse mortgage are that the loan is at a higher mortgage rate than other mortgages, so the equity in your home will decrease and there will be less value for your heirs. Other costs associated with a reverse mortgage include fees, such as an application fee, home appraisal fee and legal costs. There is also a penalty if you sell your house or move out within three years of getting the reverse mortgage. Consider other alternatives to a reverse mortgage such as finding another type of loan, for example, a conventional mortgage, credit card or line of credit, or downsize to a smaller home, rent or consider "assisted living" or another type of accommodation. Another possibility would be to sell your home to a family member and retain a life interest or consider a mortgage-financed life annuity. Talk to a professional advisor about the best option for you. See also the Financial Consumer Agency of Canada (FCAC) at **www.fcac.gc.ca** for more information on this subject.

1.3.2 HOUSING ALTERNATIVES

Each option can have complex tax rules regarding what is deductible, when and how much. Consult with your advisors when deciding what would be the best alternative for you.

Despite a desire to live at home independently, there may be times when it is impractical or unsafe for one to continue to live at home alone. The following are other housing alternatives that can be considered.

1.3.2.1 While Living at Home

A family member or friend can move in with you in order to assist with day-to-day activities and to provide companionship.

1.3.2.2 Moving in with Your Children

As much as you may want to be independent and not be a burden to your children, sometimes both practicality and finances may dictate that moving in with your children is the best option. If your children work, then this option can be supplemented with adult day care, either in the home or in an off-site facility that will provide meals, socialization and assistance with activities of daily living (ADLs).

1.3.2.3 Respite Care

This is short-term care designed to temporarily relieve care givers from their caregiving responsibilities. Respite Care can be offered on an in-home, community-based or residential basis. Respite Care, a short-term stay in a long-term care home, may be available for seniors who live alone after release from hospital who do not have a caregiver in place and cannot yet function independently.

1.3.2.4 Life Lease

A Life Lease is an alternative to owning your own home. The usual not-for-profit ownership structure and operation means affordable rent. Your equity is freed up to invest or use where you need it most — savings, travelling, family, etc. It allows for ease of estate and financial planning. For example, the entrance fee is refunded once the lease is terminated or upon death of the tenant. The building owner/operator is responsible for re-leasing the apartment.

Life Lease is different from outright purchase of a condominium in that residents are required to contribute only a portion of the cost or value of their apartment. The financial contribution is called the Entrance Fee. In return for the Entrance Fee the tenant is granted a lifetime lease on their chosen apartment. Tenants are responsible for paying a monthly occupancy expense or rent. A Life Lease may be terminated by the tenant for any reason within a particular time frame (e.g., by giving 60 days' notice). When the lease is terminated the Entrance Fee is refunded, less an administration fee.

1.3.2.5 Assisted Living

For those who need more help there are a broad range of options, from small private homes with few residents to large institutional assisted living facilities. Generally, an assisted living arrangement will provide a room or apartment to the resident, as well as housekeeping and laundry services, meals, social activities and some assistance with ADLs.

1.3.2.6 Long-Term Care Home

It is still customary for many people to think of "nursing homes" when they are considering care for aging loved ones. However, in Canada's senior care industry, you will not hear many staff refer to "nursing homes." The traditional "nursing home" in Canada is referred to as a "long term care" home, where patients will receive medical care and attention as warranted — perhaps from nurses on call around the clock.

The term "nursing home" also carries some negative connotations and as a generic catch-all term it is simply not fitting as a description of the many retirement living options available. In Canada today, senior care is increasingly adaptable and flexible, with a spectrum of options from complete independence to thorough care.

Some options you can find in retirement home living today include the following:
- Active Adult Communities allow you to live in a community with other people your own age with access to often luxurious amenities, such as a golf course, swimming pool, etc. These communities are usually age-exclusive and the age of exclusion may be as low as 50 years. That doesn't mean your grandkids can't visit! They just can't live with you.
- Independent Living also allows you to live in an exclusive community but you might also participate in communal meals and other activities. You may be protected by security and you may even want to hire your own home health care if needed.
- Congregate Living may mix together people requiring various degrees of care, including, for example, independent seniors along with those who require help with house cleaning or other regular daily activities.
- Long-term care homes offer residents care as required. Many people still think of these as "nursing homes". These may be well-staffed with nurses and other medical staff and there may be many residents who require consistent care.

It's important to note that the retirement home industry is responding to seniors' changing needs. The vast majority of retirement homes in Canada seek to treat residents with the very highest levels of respect, befitting those who have contributed so much to society in their lives. As the baby boomer generation sees their aging parents go into retirement homes, they are demanding increased options and more respectful care. In fact, they are effecting changes that they will one day benefit from when they too decide to move into a retirement home.

1.3.2.7 Hospices

Hospices are community-based volunteer organizations dedicated to helping people who are living with a life-threatening or terminal illness. Their mission is to help these people live at home—wherever that may be—or in a home-like setting as comfortably and fully as possible. They provide support to families and friends, with a range of services focused on quality of life until the end of life as well as bereavement support for loved ones. Services can include respite care and caregiver relief, complementary therapies, liaison with other community supports, transportation and friendly visiting by trained volunteers. Some communities also have residential hospices.

In medieval times, a hospice was a place of shelter or sanctuary for travellers, pilgrims and others. No journey in life is more difficult than the path followed by those suffering a life-threatening illness, so "hospice" has now become a philosophy of care built around the quality of life for the dying and those that care for them.

Hospice palliative care is active, compassionate care directed towards improving the quality of life of those with a life-threatening illness. It supports people diagnosed with a life-threatening illness and their families while living with the illness, during the time of dying and death and for a bereavement period.

1.4 TAX PLANNING: DEDUCTIONS AND CREDITS

Keep track of all of your expenses and get receipts to help you reduce your income tax payable, because the federal government uses a graduated tax system to assess personal income tax and tax credits are used in many situations rather than tax deductions to create a fairer tax system. Tax deductions create different tax benefits for higher income earners than lower income earners whereas the tax benefit received from a tax credit is the same for all income earners, usually calculated at the lowest marginal rate. An exception to that rule would be the tax credit for eligible charitable donations over $200 where the tax credit is calculated at the highest marginal rate. For more information on deductions, tax credits and tax rates, see **www.cra-arc.gc.ca**.

1.4.1 DISABILITY SUPPORTS DEDUCTION

This deduction is intended to assist taxpayers with a mental or physical impairment to attend school or work or conduct research under a grant.

Expenses can only be claimed by the person with the impairment and expenses eligible for this tax deduction are listed in the *Income Tax Act*. Examples include full- or part-time attendant care expenses for a person who qualifies for the disability tax credit and prescribed devices that help a person function with a disability, such as Braille note-takers or printers, electronic speech synthesizers, optical scanners, page-turning devices and teletypewriters. Other expenses for services that are certified by a medical practitioner as being necessary, such as job-coaching services (other than career counselling or job placement services), note-taking services, reading services, talking textbooks, tutoring services and voice recognition software are also eligible. Expenses claimed here cannot be claimed for the medical expenses or if they are reimbursed by insurance or other non-taxable payment. This list is not exhaustive. Consult your Chartered Accountant to ensure that you are claiming all eligible expenses.

1.4.2 CAREGIVER AMOUNT

A caregiver tax credit is available to individuals who care for a live-in dependant parent, grandparent or other relative who has a physical or mental infirmity. The tax credit is a percentage of a particular amount that is phased out at a prescribed level of the dependant's income.

In order to qualify, the dependant must be:
- your or your spouse's/common-law partner's child or grandchild, or
- your or your spouse's/common-law partner's aunt, uncle, brother, sister, nephew, niece, parent or grandparent and a resident in Canada (visitors are not eligible).

Also, each dependant must:
- be at least 18 years of age or older while living with you
- have a net annual income of less than the prescribed amount
- have been dependant on you because of a mental or physical infirmity, or
- in the case of a parent, be 65 years of age or older.

You cannot claim this amount if you were required to make support payments regarding that child. However, you can claim the amount if you were separated for part of the taxation year due to a marriage or relationship breakdown as long you do not claim any support payments paid to your spouse/common-law partner. Talk to your Chartered Accountant about the best option for you.

You can split the claim for the same dependant with another person up to the maximum available for that dependant.

You cannot claim the caregiver tax credit and the infirm dependant age 18 or older credit for the same dependant.

1.4.3 INFIRM DEPENDANT AGE 18 OR OLDER

This credit is available if you support an infirm dependant relative who is 18 years of age or older and a Canadian resident. This tax credit is a percentage of a certain amount and is reduced by the dependant's income over a certain threshold until it is completely phased out at a maximum income threshold.

The dependant relative must be your or your spouse's/common-law partner's child or grandchild who is 18 years of age or older and is mentally or physically impaired. You can claim this amount for more than one person where certain conditions are met if the person is:

- your or your spouse's/common-law partner's aunt, uncle, brother, sister, nephew, niece, parent or grandparent and resident in Canada (visitors are not eligible)
- 18 years of age or older
- dependent on you either alone or with others for support
- a Canadian resident at any time in the year.

The credit is not available if you can claim a caregiver amount as discussed above in section 1.4.2 for that dependant. You can claim this credit if you are also claiming the eligible dependant credit but you cannot claim this credit if someone else is claiming the eligible dependant credit.

You can claim this credit for each eligible dependant.

You cannot claim this amount if you were required to make support payments regarding that child. However you can claim the amount if you were separated for part of the taxation year due to a marriage or relationship breakdown as long as you do not claim any support payments paid to your spouse/common-law partner. Talk to your Chartered Accountant about the best option for you.

You can split the claim for the same dependant with another person up to the maximum available for that dependant.

1.4.3.1 Family Caregiver Tax Credit

Effective for 2012 and subsequent taxation years, the 2011 Federal Budget and legislation proposes to introduce an enhanced, non-refundable 15% tax credit on an amount of $2,000 to existing credits called the Family Caregiver Tax Credit to provide tax relief to caregivers of related dependants, including spouses, common-law partners and minor children. The Family Caregiver Tax Credit amount of $2,000 will be indexed for 2013 and subsequent taxation years. Consult your Chartered Accountant regarding how the changes could reduce your taxes.

1.4.4 MEDICAL EXPENSES TAX CREDIT

You can claim medical expenses for any 12-month period that ends in the tax year for which you are filing your tax return and can claim expenses for yourself, your spouse, common-law partner and minor children. The expenses must exceed the lesser of a prescribed threshold amount and 3% of your net income. Expenses for other dependants can be claimed to a maximum $10,000 if they also exceed the minimum amount prescribed by formula. Effective for 2011 and subsequent taxation years, the 2011 Federal Budget and legislation proposes to eliminate the $10,000 ceiling on eligible expenses that can be claimed for the Medical Expenses Tax Credit for a dependent relative.

Dependants include children, grandchildren, parents, grandparents, brothers, sisters, aunts, uncles, nieces or nephews that depend on you for support.

Medical expenses for a deceased taxpayer can be claimed for any 24-month period that includes the date of death.

Medical expenses that can be claimed for tax purposes are prescribed in the *Income Tax Act* and its Regulations.

Expenses that are eligible for the medical expenses tax credit include:
- medical and dental services
- full-time attendant care at home or nursing home care
- attendant care
- group home care
- school or institution care
- ambulance services
- transportation services
- certain travel expenses
- artificial limbs, wheelchairs and other supportive devices
- diapers, catheters and other incontinence products
- eyeglasses
- oxygen tent, insulin, related equipment and shots for anaemia prescribed by a doctor
- guide dogs and related expenses
- bone marrow and organ transplant related expenses
- home alterations, construction and renovations to assist a disabled person

- hearing and speech loss rehabilitative therapy
- sign language interpretation or real-time captioning services
- note-taking services
- voice recognition software
- reading services to help a blind person
- deaf-blind intervening services
- moving expenses
- alterations to a residential driveway to provide for access to a bus for a patient who has a severe and prolonged mobility impairment
- costs to adapt a van for a wheelchair
- training courses related to caring for a disabled person
- therapy for a disabled person
- tutoring services for a person with a learning disability or a mental impairment
- various devices or equipment that are prescribed by regulation
- prescribed medications
- diagnostic services such as laboratory or radiological
- dentures
- private health services plan premium
- expenses incurred for gluten-free foods
- medical devices or drugs under Health Canada's Special Access Programme
- medically required marihuana as permitted under the *Marihuana Medical Access Regulations* or the *Controlled Drugs and Substances Act*.

This list is not exhaustive. Consult your Chartered Accountant to be sure that you are claiming all the medical expenses that you are entitled to.

1.4.5 DISABILITY TAX CREDIT

An individual is entitled to a non-refundable disability tax credit if they are certi-fied by a prescribed medical professional as being blind or as suffering from a "severe and prolonged impairment in physical or mental functions." This impair-ment must "markedly restrict" the ability to perform a basic activity of daily living all, or substantially all, of the time, or must "markedly restrict" the ability if not for therapy. The therapy must be administered a minimum of three times a week for at least 14 hours per week.

In order to qualify for the disability tax credit, a medical certificate on Form T2201 must be filed. The certificate can be filed at any time during the year. Filing

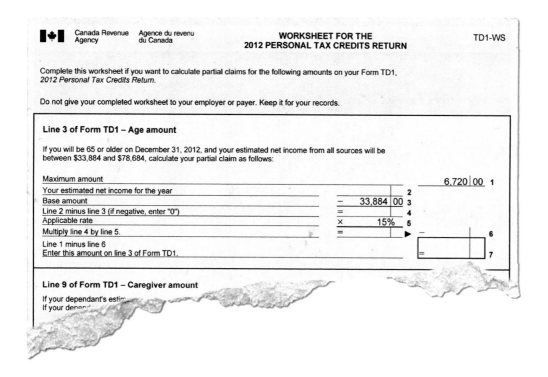

the form before filing the tax return may save time in assessing the return because the CRA has the opportunity to review the certificate and status ahead of time. If you have a disability and have not had it certified by the applicable prescribed medical professional you may, depending on the disability, be able to request an amendment to a previous tax year up to a maximum of 10 calendar years.

Recent changes have been made to ensure that a taxpayer can file a Notice of Objection, subject to prescribed time limits, when the CRA has determined an applicant is not eligible for the Disability Tax Credit. Prior to the legislative changes, a taxpayer could not file a Notice of Objection of a Notice of Assessment or Reassessment of their income tax return that stated that there was no tax payable. Eligibility for the Disability Tax Credit is fundamental to establishing a Registered Disability Savings Plan. Time limits apply, so consult your Chartered Accountant.

Prescribed medical professionals include audiologists, occupational therapists, medical doctors, optometrists, physiotherapists, psychologists, and speech-language pathologists.

Basic daily living activities include the ability to dress, eliminate, feed, hear, speak, walk or mentally function for everyday living.

An individual may receive a medical certificate if they are "significantly restricted" where they are not markedly restricted in any one activity but the cumulative effect of two or more basic activities of daily living significantly restrict their abilities.

CHAPTER 2

PLANNING FOR YOUR ESTATE

2.1 ESTATE PLANNING

Estate planning is a process designed to help you manage and preserve your assets while you are alive, and to conserve and control their distribution after your death according to your goals and objectives. Your age, health, wealth, lifestyle, life stage, goals and many other factors determine your particular estate-planning needs. For example, you may have a small estate and may be concerned only that certain people receive particular assets or you may have a large estate and your foremost goal is minimizing any potential tax liability. While there are no estate taxes in Canada, under the *Income Tax Act*, a person is deemed to dispose of all of their property at fair market value immediately before death, which could trigger tax liability, such as capital gains and recapture where capital property is depreciated and any additions or improvements in the year are added to the selling cost or fair market value. Registered Retirement Savings Plans (RRSPs), Registered Retirement Income Funds (RRIFs), Tax-Free Savings Accounts (TFSA) and similar plans must be collapsed. A Chartered Accountant and estate lawyer should be consulted to determine the appropriate estate plan. A Chartered Accountant can also prepare the terminal returns and do the tax planning going forward. If you own assets in a foreign jurisdiction, consult with a lawyer of that jurisdiction as to how the local law would affect your property at death. For example, you may be subject to estate tax if you own property in the United States at the time of death. Also, if you decide to gift U.S. property during your lifetime you may be subject to gift tax. This is a complex area, subject to exemptions, tax treaties, tax credits and filing deadlines. Professional advice from an accountant and lawyer of the particular jurisdiction is recommended.

Estate planning is not only for the rich. It can be used by anyone to ensure that financial concerns and goals are addressed after death. That may include providing for dependants, avoiding probate or reducing tax.

Estate planning may be as simple as writing a will (the cornerstone of any estate plan) or as complex as executing trusts and exploring sophisticated tax or estate planning techniques.

Some of the purposes of estate planning are:

1. To decide how a person's assets are to be distributed at death;

2. To minimize tax owing at death; and

3. To have a way of funding taxes at death.

2.1.1 SPECIAL CIRCUMSTANCES

Estate planning may also be important if:
- there are minor or special-needs children
- your spouse is uncomfortable or inexperienced with handling financial matters
- you own property in more than one jurisdiction
- you own special property, such as artwork or collectibles
- you own certain property such as a qualified fishing property, farming property or qualified small business shares that may be eligible for a capital gains exemption
- you own a business.

Passing a family-owned business to the next generation can be a very important challenge. Some of the objectives to be considered include:
- Who is going to control the business?
- Who is going to participate in its future growth?
- Who is going to receive its income?
- What provisions are to be made for the surviving spouse who was not active in the business?

Make a will and review it periodically as well as when major life events occur

These topics will be further discussed in this section, but it is important that you consult with your Chartered Accountant to discuss your estate plan.

2.2 MAKING A TESTAMENTARY WILL

A will is a legal document which expresses your desires as to whom you wish to benefit from your estate, how much you want to give them and exactly how you wish your estate to be distributed. You may also wish to name guardians for your minor children in your will. You can pass property to your beneficiaries outside of a will. Some of the reasons to do this include the ability to reduce probate fees/taxes; defer tax liability on some *inter vivos* transfers (which we will discuss in the trusts section); and to keep as much of your affairs private as possible which does not happen when a will is probated. It is also possible to own property with another person, in joint ownership of a property, which will allow the property of a deceased joint owner to pass outside your will to the surviving owners (note that "joint ownership" does not exist under Quebec law). The disadvantage to these alternatives is that you give up some or all control of the property as opposed to maintaining control and benefits of the property if your assets are bequeathed in your will.

Everyone should have a testamentary will to provide for how you wish your estate to be divided upon your death. As in the case of the documents previously mentioned, a will should be drafted by a lawyer familiar with the laws of the province in which the person making the will resides or real property is located. If there is no will, the applicable succession legislation governs. The estate is distributed in accordance to a prescribed list of next of kin, which may not coincide with your wishes.

Matters to consider when drafting a will include:
- minor children and/or children from a previous marriage
- beneficiaries with special needs
- ownership of significant assets and the desire to minimize probate taxes
- goals such as controlling the management and distribution of property after death
- the chance that the will may be contested after death

- desire for a specific asset (such as a coin or stamp collection) to go to a certain person
- desire that heirs be disinherited
- charitable donations.

Despite the existence of a will, a spouse is entitled to a minimum amount of the estate in many jurisdictions, called a preferential share, if the deceased did not adequately provide for them under the will and an election is made in a timely manner.

Wills of a husband and wife that name each other as the beneficiary often include a survivorship clause in the event that they die in a common accident or one spouse dies shortly after the other. The clause will provide that if the beneficiary does not survive for a reasonable short period of time, such as 30 days, then each estate is distributed to other beneficiaries.

> Probate makes your will a public document

What if there is no will? In that case, the succession legislation of the applicable province or territory governs the administration of the estate and it is distributed in accordance to the legislative scheme of the *Act*. In most jurisdictions, the spouse is entitled to a preferential share and then the children are entitled to a portion if there is more than the preferential share in the estate.

Disinheritance involves stating that someone is not entitled to inherit even though they would otherwise be a rightful heir. Typically heirs include a husband or wife, children and possibly other relatives. Remember too that leaving a child out of a will may not succeed in disinheriting that child. All jurisdictions provide for a claim for support for dependants that can prove that they are entitled to financial assistance from the estate. Consult an experienced estate planning lawyer.

2.2.1 HOW TO MAKE A WILL

Although not recommended, a will may legally be prepared without a lawyer. It may be drafted with the help of a guidebook or software, or by purchasing a prescribed form in an office supply store or online. To make a legally valid will, you must be at least of the age of majority or older and of sound mind. The age of majority is 18 in Alberta, Manitoba, Ontario, Prince Edward Island, Quebec, and Saskatchewan and 19 in British Columbia, New Brunswick, Newfoundland and

Labrador, Northwest Territories, Nova Scotia, Nunavut, and Yukon. The minimum age requirement is waived when it is made in contemplation of marriage in all jurisdictions except Newfoundland and Labrador. The marriage must occur for the will to be valid. There are usually special provisions for members of the armed forces and seamen. A minor in Quebec may also make a will for property that is of little value.

A person must be of sound mind, that is, aware of the scope of their property, all of the potential beneficiaries who would normally be included in the will and how being included or excluded would affect them. Also, the will must be in writing and meet the legislative requirements of the applicable jurisdiction for formal execution, reflect your true wishes and be made without undue influence. Proper execution includes signing and acknowledging the will in the presence of adult witnesses who will not benefit by anything under the will. While drafting a will on your own will cost less, nuances and potential changes in federal and provincial law should at least cause you to consider utilizing the services of a lawyer who specializes in estate-planning matters.

The required formalities will depend on the applicable jurisdiction and the type of will that is made. Types of wills include conventional wills (formal), holographic wills (informal and handwritten) and international wills. Legal advice is recommended when making a will to ensure that it reflects your true desires and your expectations as to how it is carried out will be met.

2.2.2 MULTIPLE WILLS

You can have more than one will. The courts have accepted the use of multiple wills in Canada to reduce probate fees/taxes. In Ontario, this fee or tax is called estate administration tax. You may have one will that will be subject to probate and another will to pass property that is not subject to probate. Clients may also have created trusts, one of the benefits of which is to pass property outside of the estate. See Section 2.4.5 of this *Guide*.

2.2.3 PROBATE

A will does not necessarily have to be probated. It is usually done to assure a third party that the executors have authority to deal with the estate, that the property will be free of any beneficiary claims and that they are getting good title. Financial institutions will often require a will to be probated before they transfer any assets to the executors to ensure that they will not be liable in case the executor gives any of the property to the wrong person.

The probate process can take a varied amount of time depending on the size of the estate, the location of beneficiaries, any contests made to the will and applicable law. An Affidavit of Witness may be required for a probate application. This may have been executed by a witness at the time you signed your will. If not, they may need to be located in order to execute an Affidavit of Witness if a probate application is being made. Probate fees/taxes are generally assessed on the value of the estate that is being passed through the will and they vary across the country. The fees/tax may change, so talk to your Chartered Accountant.

Jurisdiction	Value of Estate	Probate Fee/Tax
Alberta	Less than or equal to $10,000	$25
British Columbia	Less than or equal to $25,000	Nil
	More than $25,000 and less than or equal to $50,000	$6 for every $1,000 rounded up
	More than $50,000	$14 for every $1,000 rounded up
Manitoba	Less than or equal to $10,000	$70
	More than $10,000	$7 for every $1,000 rounded up
New Brunswick	Less than or equal to $5,000	$25
	More than $5,000 and less than or equal to $10,000	$50
	More than $10,000 and less than or equal to $15,000	$75
	More than $15,000 and less than or equal to $20,000	$100
	More than $20,000	$5 for every $1,000 rounded up
Newfoundland and Labrador	All estates	.005 × for every $100 rounded up and $85
Northwest Territories	Less than or equal to $10,000	$25
	More than $10,000 and less than or equal to $25,000	$100
	More than $25,000 and less than or equal to $125,000	$200
	More than $125,000 and less than or equal to $250,000	$300
	More than $250,000	$400
Nova Scotia	Less than or equal to $10,000	$77.00
	More than $10,000 and less than or equal to $25,000	$193.61
	More than $25,000 and less than or equal to $50,000	$322.21
	More than $50,000 and less than or equal to $100,000	$902.03
	More than $100,000	$902.03 plus $15.23 for every $1,000 rounded up

Jurisdiction	Value of Estate	Probate Fee/Tax
Nunavut	Less than or equal to $25,000	$100
	More than $25,000 and less than or equal to $125,000	$200
	More than $125,000 and less than or equal to $250,000	$300
	More than $250,000	$400
Ontario	Less than or equal to $50,000	$5 for every $1,000 rounded up
	More than $50,000	$15 for every $1,000 rounded up
Prince Edward Island	Less than or equal to $10,000	$50
	More than $10,000 and less than or equal to $25,000	$100
	More than $25,000 and less than or equal to $50,000	$200
	More than $50,000 and less than or equal to $100,000	$400
	More than $100,000	$4 for every $1,000 rounded up
Quebec	N/A	Nil
Saskatchewan	All estates	$7 for every $1,000 rounded up
Yukon	Less than or equal to $25,000	Nil
	More than $25,000	$140

This list is not exhaustive and does not include miscellaneous fees like photocopying or other fees.

Where there is no will, probate is also required for the court to appoint a representative, usually called an administrator (estate trustee in Ontario).

Probate also makes the will a public document. The estate pays the probate costs, thereby reducing the amount of money going to the heirs.

2.2.4 CHOOSING BENEFICIARIES

A Chartered Accountant can help you plan for the financial needs of your dependants and a lawyer can draft the proper estate-planning documents to ensure your wishes are followed. When choosing beneficiaries those who may need to be considered include:

Spouse: In the event of your illness or death, it is important to ensure that a spouse continues to have access to your shared assets. To ensure proper titling of ownership, individuals are encouraged to seek legal advice.

Common-law partner: In many jurisdictions across Canada, many rights enjoyed by a spouse have been extended to a common-law partner, although the rights vary among the jurisdictions and applicable legislation. In Quebec, the *Civil Code* does not recognize common-law partners for the purpose of support among other matrimonial rights. However, a 2010 Court of Appeal case found that the *Civil Code* discriminated against a common-law partner for the purpose of support. There are also various treatments of matrimonial property across the other jurisdictions where property rights are not usually extended to common-law partners, although there are exceptions. In succession law, most provinces do not extend the same rights of married spouses to common-law partners where the other spouse/common-law partner dies intestate, although there are exceptions. Consult an estate lawyer.

The *Income Tax Act* defines for tax purposes a common-law partner as either a parent with the other partner of a child or a person who has cohabited with the other person in a conjugal relationship for a minimum period of one year. Legal advice is recommended.

Former spouse/common-law partner: Your advisor can help you arrange an automatic transfer arrangement to ensure spousal support continues during your illness. Spousal support generally ends upon the death of the payor spouse/common-law partner although it is possible to provide for a spouse/common-law partner if desired. They may also have a claim from the estate as a dependant if they are not adequately provided for in the will. Consult your advisor.

Same-sex partner: In Canada, same-sex partners are entitled to many of the same rights and benefits as common-law partners in Canada, including recognition under the *Income Tax Act*, *Canada Pension Plan* and other statutes. The federal *Civil Marriage Act* was amended in 2005 to permit same-sex couples to marry.

Child support: The death of a payor may be addressed in a separation or similar agreement where the parties agree to designate a child as a beneficiary under an insurance policy to provide child support payments after death. A taxable monthly orphan benefit is provided through CPP/QPP to your minor children if an application is made in writing on a timely basis and you are a qualified CPP contributor. Again, a claim as a dependant may be made if a minor child is not adequately provided for in your will. Since each family's situation is different, it's best to seek legal advice.

Children with special needs: A child, even a grown one, with physical or mental disabilities can require special planning.

Other dependants: You will likely have to make special arrangements if you wish to provide for your parents or other family members during an illness or after your death.

A will helps you express your wishes as to how you would like your estate divided up and distributed. Generally it is your choice to benefit someone or leave them out of your will. However, there are exceptions.

Legislation across the country provides that dependants can apply for a court order for support or maintenance if they have not been adequately provided for in the will and can demonstrate they were dependent on the deceased. Legislation generally applies to spouses and minor children although the definitions for each and the applicable test can vary. For example, some jurisdictions include common-law partners. Many provide that a former spouse who was receiving support is considered a dependant. In Quebec, the right exists for a dependant called a creditor of support, who is defined as an eligible heir, legatee or person who did not exercise their right to support prior to the person's death. Time limits apply to make an application. Legal advice is recommended.

As well, legislation generally gives spouses a preferential share of the net estate or the estate's net value, depending on the jurisdiction, if they are not adequately provided for in the will. The definition of spouse varies.

Legislation generally recognizes a deceased's children to include children born out of wedlock as well as adopted children. Consideration should also be given if there are step-children that you wish to include.

Specific gifts to individuals should be clearly identified and the individuals should be specifically named.

Consideration should also be given to whether you wish to make direct beneficiary designations for on certain instruments such as registered retirement savings plans, tax-free savings accounts and insurance policies. If you do so, they will fall outside of your will. Consult your advisor.

2.2.5 GUARDIANSHIP OF YOUR CHILDREN

The guardianship of your children is an important matter to consider during an incapacitating illness or after your death. The surviving parent will be sole guardian where the other parent dies if they are both custodial parents. However, guardianship will not automatically pass to the other parent if they did not already have custodial rights. You can name a guardian in your will to care for your children. However, the court may appoint another person if they believe that to do so would be in the best interest of the child.

Choosing the person who will care for your child if you are unable to do so is an extremely important decision. Some issues to consider:

- Who loves and cares about the children?
- Who do the children love and respect?
- Who do you trust?
- Who is financially and emotionally able to take on added responsibilities?
- Who is willing to take on the guardianship responsibility?
- Who is honest and dependable?

Consider also:

- Is it best to name the guardian in your will?
- Talk to the person to ensure that they are willing and able.
- Some parents name one guardian to care for children and a different guardian to oversee the children's assets and finances.
- Single parents may choose to name the child's other parent, even if they do not have legal custody.
- The court has the final authority and will look at all relevant factors in determining what is in the best interests of the child.

Talk with a prospective guardian about:

- The responsibility they are taking on in agreeing to care for your children.
- Your wishes for their upbringing, including your religion, the education you would like them to receive, and other important matters.
- Financial resources that will be available, including life insurance, disability insurance, savings, investments, etc.

A Chartered Accountant can help you plan for the financial needs of your dependants, and a lawyer can draft the proper estate-planning documents to ensure your wishes are followed.

> **The Sandwich Generation: Approximately 30% of Canadians aged 45–64 have both aging parents and children under 25**
>
> Statistics Canada 2002 General Survey

> **Life expectancy in Canada increased by 2.3 years in a decade from 78.4 years between 1995 and 1997 to 80.7 years between 2005 and 2007**
>
> Statistics Canada: *The Daily* February 23, 2010

2.2.6 PERSONAL REPRESENTATIVE

Choosing a personal representative (executor, estate trustee or liquidator, depending on the jurisdiction) to administer your will is a very important decision. Often times an adult child is chosen. An alternative should be chosen in case your first choice is not able or willing to carry out the duties.

Choosing who will administer your will (the executor in all jurisdictions except Ontario (estate trustee) and Quebec (liquidator)) is an important aspect in making a will. For the purpose of this discussion, the term "personal representative" will be used for the person administering your estate.

The person who makes a will is called the testator. When making your will, choose a person to be your personal representative whom you know will carry out your wishes. This person does not need to be a family member or next of kin. Ask yourself who is the best person you know who is capable of carrying out the duties as required, who is someone you trust implicitly and who is someone who will carry out your desired wishes. Acting as a personal representative involves great responsibility in dealing with your assets, meeting deadlines for carrying out certain tasks as well as meeting income tax filing obligations. While it is possible to make a valid will on your own, legal advice is recommended to ensure that your desires are properly reflected in your will.

2.2.7 LEAVING THE CHOICE TO THE GOVERNMENT

A person who does not plan for the distribution of their estate and dies without a will is said to have died intestate (without a will). The probate court will appoint a next of kin to administer your estate as dictated by the applicable succession legislation. If there is no next of kin the public trustee, public guardian and trustee or other public office will be appointed to administer your estate for a fee. The person appointed by the court may not be the person you would choose and by not having a will you lose control of both who administers your estate and who receives the assets under your will.

Generally the representative of a deceased who dies intestate and is appointed by the court is called the administrator and the representative of a deceased who is appointed under the will is called the executor. Legislation across the country regarding succession law is particular to its jurisdiction and terminology sometimes varies. For the purpose of this *Guide*, as discussed earlier, the administrator or executor will be called the "personal representative".

2.3 PLANNING FOR YOUR ASSETS AND YOUR PROPERTY

Take inventory of what you own. You can either be the sole owner, own something jointly with your spouse or another person, or own property with another person as a tenant in common. If you are the sole owner, you can generally deal with your assets as you choose. Joint ownership gives the survivor(s) rights to the property of another joint owner when they die (note that "joint ownership" does not exist under Quebec law). If you are a tenant in common, you own a certain percentage of the property. This interest can be passed to your heirs at death. You may also have a beneficial interest in a trust. If the interest only exists while you are alive, this is called a life interest.

> **Do you know how your assets are owned?**

Assets that you own alone can be bequeathed to your heirs as you express in your will.

2.3.1 ASSETS OWNED JOINTLY WITH A SPOUSE

Assets that are owned jointly between spouses pass full title to the surviving spouse.

2.3.2 FAMILY PROPERTY

Provincial legislation generally recognizes income and property gained during a marriage as family or community property. Property rights in many provinces apply to married spouses only but may also apply to common-law partners. A "spouse" as defined in the applicable legislation can take a preferential share where the testator (the person making the will) does not provide for a minimum amount under the will. Time limits apply for making this election. Check with your lawyer on whether your will can be thwarted by the applicable legislation.

> **Beneficiary choices should be reviewed regularly**
>
> **Are your assets titled to produce the outcome you want?**

2.3.3 ASSETS HELD IN TRUST

Assets titled by a trust generally are not included in the probate process and therefore go directly to the intended recipients on whatever schedule the trust directs.

Trusts have the following advantages:

- generally avoid probate (court supervision)
- maintain privacy (compared to probated wills, which are recorded with the court and open to the public)
- provide for control of assets both during life and after death
- may provide tax benefits
- can be structured to take care of your family after your death.

See the section on Trusts (Section 2.4.5) for further details on different types of trusts that can be used to pass property outside of a will.

2.4 PASSING ASSETS OUTSIDE OF THE ESTATE

You may wish to pass assets outside of your estate, which can be done in several ways. As mentioned above, joint ownership gives joint owners the right of survivorship. There could be difficulties associated with joint ownership because lawsuits, liens or divorce (all of which could have negative income tax consequences) of the other owner(s) can affect the interests of all owners. (Note that "joint ownership" does not exist under Quebec law.)

Assets that are titled in your name only but have a named beneficiary (that is, left to someone other than your estate) will be distributed directly to that beneficiary. Examples include Registered Retirement Savings Plans, Registered Retirement Income Funds, Registered Pension Plans, Tax-free Savings Accounts and life insurance policies that designate the beneficiary or beneficiaries. You should review your beneficiary choices regularly to ensure they are up-to-date, particularly if you have recently been widowed or divorced.

Many individuals name their spouse or other family members as beneficiaries of their retirement plans. These retirement plans may consist of Registered Retirement Pension Plans, Registered Retirement Income Funds or other tax qualified or pension benefits. Qualified beneficiaries can receive amounts on a tax deferred basis if they are transferred to their respective plan or fund and elections are filed on a timely basis. Seek the assistance of a Chartered Accountant and estate planning lawyer.

2.4.1 REGISTERED RETIREMENT SAVINGS PLANS

If you have a Registered Retirement Savings Plan (RRSP), it has either begun paying retirement benefits (matured) or has not begun paying retirement benefits (unmatured).

2.4.1.1 Unmatured RRSP

You are called the annuitant of an unmatured RRSP if you are continuing to make contributions to your RRSP. When an annuitant dies, they are deemed to receive into their income in the year of death an amount equal to the RRSP fair market value immediately before death, subject to the following exceptions. A spouse/common-law partner who is directly designated as the sole beneficiary in the annuitant's RRSP can direct the RRSP issuer to transfer the property on or before the calendar taxation year-end of the year following the year of the annuitant's death into their own eligible RRSP or RRIF. The amount is then included in their income rather than the annuitant's. Where the previous situation does not apply and the RRSP property qualifies as a refund of premiums to a qualified beneficiary, the deceased annuitant's legal representative can claim a deduction for the amount of the RRSP property and it is included in the income of the qualified beneficiary. On a tax-deferred basis, a qualified beneficiary can transfer the refund of premiums to an eligible RRSP or RRIF within 60 days after the calendar year-end of the year they received the funds.

2.4.1.2 Matured RRSP

You are called the annuitant of a matured RRSP if you are not making contributions to your RRSP and have made arrangements to receive a retirement income from your accumulated investment. When an annuitant dies, they are deemed to have received the fair market value of the remaining RRSP payments immediately before death. This amount is included in the annuitant's income in the year of death except in the following situations:

- The plan continues where the annuitant named their spouse/common-law partner directly on the RRSP contract as the sole beneficiary.

- Where another beneficiary is named with the spouse/common-law partner, the portion attributed to the spouse/common-law partner continues under the plan and the fair market value of the other portion is included in the deceased's income in the year of death.
- If there is no direct designation and the spouse/common-law partner is named under the will as the sole beneficiary or is named as the sole beneficiary of the estate, then the spouse/common-law partner and the legal representative can jointly elect by writing a letter to the CRA that the spouse/common-law partner intends to become the successor annuitant under the RRSP. The RRSP annuity payor should also be given a copy of the letter.

The legal representative can also reduce the amount that is included in the deceased annuitant's income in the year of death where a financially dependent child or grandchild is qualified to receive an amount as a refund of premiums. The recipient can defer the tax payable on the RRSP amount received by transferring the property to a qualified fund or plan or to a registered issuer to purchase a qualified annuity within 60 days after the calendar year-end of receiving the refund of premiums.

Due to the recent economic downturn the *Income Tax Act* recognizes the inequity where the post death amount that is distributed is less than the fair market value of the investment immediately before death. The decrease in value can be carried back and applied against the amount of the income inclusion in the year of death.

2.4.2 REGISTERED RETIREMENT INCOME FUNDS

You cannot continue to contribute to an RRSP after December 31 of the year you turn 71 years old. You must begin to make withdrawals the following year. You can transfer a mature RRSP to a Registered Retirement Income Fund (RRIF) so that you are only taxed up to the actual amount withdrawn rather than collapsing the RRSP and being taxed on the whole amount of the RRSP. A RRIF can continue for the rest of your life.

When the annuitant of a RRIF dies, they are deemed to receive the fair market value of the amount immediately before death except in the following situations.

The RRIF continues where the annuitant named their spouse/common-law partner directly on the RRIF contract or in their will as the successor annuitant and the payments are taxable as they are received by the successor annuitant. Or, the spouse/common-law partner is named as the sole beneficiary in the RRIF contract and directs the RRIF administrator by the end of the calendar year-end following the year the annuitant died to transfer all the RRIF property to an eligible plan or fund. The legal representative can also reduce the amount that is included in the deceased annuitant's income in the year of death where a qualified beneficiary receives a designated benefit. The beneficiary can defer the tax payable on the RRIF property received by transferring the property to a qualified fund or plan or to a registered issuer to purchase a qualified annuity within 60 days after the calendar year-end of receiving the RRSP property. RRIF property that is payable to the estate may qualify as a designated benefit where a qualified beneficiary is a beneficiary of the estate and the personal representative and the beneficiary jointly elect in prescribed form that the amount is designated as a designated benefit.

2.4.3 RRIF AND RRSP ROLLOVERS TO A REGISTERED DISABILITY SAVINGS PLAN

Draft legislation released August 27, 2010 provides for a tax-deferred transfer (rollover) of certain RRSP, RRIF or RPP amounts to a deceased's financially dependent child's or grandchild's Registered Disability Savings Plan (RDSP) for deaths that occur after March 3, 2010. A child is considered eligible if, because of their infirmity, they were financially dependent on the deceased at the time of their death. The proceeds will be considered eligible if they are a refund of premiums from an RRSP, eligible RRIF amount or RPP lump sum payment (except from actuarial surplus) that the eligible child or grandchild receives as a consequence of their parent's or grandparent's death. A specified RDSP payment can be paid to the child's or grandchild's RDSP after June 2011 and must be designated by the eligible child and the RDSP holder as a specified RDSP payment when the payment is made. The RDSP is included in the child's income for the taxation year when the payment is made in the year or within 60 days of that taxation year. A corresponding deduction equal to the eligible proceeds that were included in computing their taxable income for the year will be permitted. The specified RDSP payment amount will be included in the child's income when it is withdrawn. As this is draft legislation, changes could be made before it becomes law.

When the beneficiary of an RDSP dies, all Canada Disability Savings Grants (CDSGs), Canada Disability Savings Bond (CDSBs) and related investments that were made in the 10 years prior to the beneficiary's death must be repaid. The amount in excess of original contributions is taxable and is included either in the income of the beneficiary in the year of death or the estate. The beneficiary of a RDSP is the only person who is entitled to the proceeds from the plan. The savings and interest earned in the plan are transferred to the beneficiary's estate. Often a parent or legal representative will be the holder of the RDSP for the beneficiary. If you are a holder, you may consider naming your spouse or common-law partner as a joint holder so that in the event of your death the plan can continue uninterrupted.

2.4.4 LIFE INSURANCE

There are various types of life insurance policies that are designed to meet different needs. The following discussion highlights the basic products. You should get professional advice to ensure that the policy you choose meets your individual desires.

Previous employee benefits should be investigated

One of the most common reasons for buying life insurance is to replace the loss of income that would occur in the event of your death. When you die and your pay cheques stop, your family may be left with extremely limited resources. Proceeds from a life insurance policy make cash available to support your family upon your death.

Basically there are two types of life insurance policies—term and permanent.

2.4.4.1 Term

Term policies provide life insurance protection for a specific period of time or to a specified age. If a policy holder dies during the coverage period, the beneficiary receives the policy death benefit. Premiums generally stay the same during the term of the policy but increase upon renewal of the policy. For example, premiums would rise at five year intervals on a five-year renewal policy.

2.4.4.2 Permanent

Term to 100: This type of policy is usually considered a permanent plan but has no or very small cash value after a length of time and does not pay dividends. It also may have limited non-forfeiture values. Non-forfeiture options give policy holders choices if they stop paying premiums. Premiums tend to be lower than for a whole life policy.

Whole life: With this policy, you generally make equal premium payments for life. The death benefit and cash value are predetermined and guaranteed. The death benefit may be enhanced in participating policies that pay dividends, although not guaranteed. The policy owner's only action after purchase of the policy is to pay the fixed premium.

Universal life: This is a type of interest-rate sensitive policy where interest rates can be adjusted over time. Premiums could decrease where interest rates increase and conversely premiums could increase where interest rates decrease. There are two parts to a universal life policy—an investment account and life insurance. Whether earnings on the investment account are guaranteed will depend on the chosen investment. Income earned in the investment account is generally exempt from income tax. A policy holder has flexibility on the amount of premiums and death benefit, subject to limitations.

Variable life: Usually, premiums are guaranteed. The cash values fluctuate depending on how an investment fund or other index performs. Death benefits may be either guaranteed or be dependent on the fund's performance, but no less than a guaranteed minimum.

Group life insurance is often available to employees through their employers or unions.

Once you have reviewed all beneficiary designations on insurance policies to ensure they are current and appropriate, there are other questions to consider.

Is anyone dependent on your income?

For instance, are life insurance benefits taxable? Benefits are generally not taxable to a beneficiary, however, there are situations where tax consequences arise. For example, earned interest on accumulated dividends that are left on deposit is taxable.

How can life insurance be used to cover expenses related to a terminal illness? It is best to consult a financial advisor before selling or surrendering part or all of a life insurance policy. Before taking any steps, consider your dependants' needs for the benefit after your death, and remember:

If a policy has accumulated a cash value over the years, you can borrow against it, but borrowed amounts must be paid back. If they are not, the amounts plus interest are subtracted from the death benefit.

Don't let insurance premiums lapse. Make sure you make arrangements to pay your premium

If there is an accelerated benefits or living benefits rider, it can be used when a life insured is suffering from an ongoing terminal illness. The insurance company usually pays a portion of the benefit to the patient, subject to a maximum limit.

2.4.4.3 Beneficiaries

The beneficiary usually can choose how the death benefit of a life insurance policy will be paid and should review the policy for the available options.

CAUTION: It is extremely important to consider the options of any distributions and their tax implications. Before making any decisions on these options, seek the assistance of a competent advisor. It is important, also, that the option you select is appropriate for your family situation. Evaluate options in light of what the family's needs and objectives are going to be. As a result, it might be prudent to delay making a decision for a period of time.

When making a claim, the insurance company will need a copy of the death certificate, proof of the beneficiary's identity and will want to know that the beneficiary understands the available payment options. If a life insurance policy cannot be found, but a beneficiary believes there is one, they can contact the Canadian Life and Health Insurance Association at **www.clhia.ca/index_en_red.htm** who will notify all member life insurance companies of the deceased. If one of the member insurance companies has a policy, they will contact the beneficiary.

2.4.5 TRUSTS

A trust is a legal relationship in which one party, the trustee, has legal ownership of assets that have been transferred to the trust by the person (settlor) who established the trust, which assets are to be managed for the benefit of the beneficiaries of the trust.

Trustees must manage the trust to a certain standard of care and duties. Their powers and other administrative matters are governed by the trust document, as well as applicable trust legislation. There are also *Income Tax Act* provisions that the trustee must adhere to in administering a trust.

Trusts of various kinds are frequently used in personal financial planning and in estate planning. Clients with sizeable estates are likely to have established various trusts either during their lifetime or to become effective upon their death.

2.4.5.1 Some Basic Terminology
- **Testamentary Trust**—A trust usually established in a person's will and becoming active upon death of the testator.
- **Inter Vivos Trust**—A trust established during a settlor's lifetime.
- **Revocable Trust**—A trust that can be terminated or modified by the settlor.
- **Irrevocable Trust**—A trust that cannot be modified by the settlor for any reason.

Testamentary Trust

A testamentary trust is usually created at the time of a person's death and is found in the will. Testamentary trusts are taxed at graduated tax rates rather than at the highest marginal rate, as is the case of *inter vivos* trusts.

Inter Vivos Trust

An *inter vivos* trust is created by a person while they are alive. A transfer of property to a trust is considered a taxable event which must be reported by the individual on their tax return. The transfer may result in a capital gain, capital loss, recapture or terminal loss, depending on the type of property transferred and whether or not it has been depreciated. Individuals should be aware that if they settle a trust for a related individual who is under 18, paid out of the trust will be taxed to the individual who settled the trust. Capital gains will be taxed to the related minor.

Income that is retained by the trust will be taxed to the trust. Income earned in an *inter vivos* trust is taxed at the highest federal marginal rate. *Inter vivos* trusts have a calendar year-end and are generally required to file a trust return within 90 days of that year-end.

Beware of the tax on split income, known as "kiddie tax", which taxes at the highest marginal rate (29% federally plus provincially) certain trust income and certain taxable dividend income that is distributed through a trust to a related beneficiary under the age of 18 at the end of the calendar year. There are also other types of income allocated to a related beneficiary that can be caught by the kiddie tax. Consult your Chartered Accountant.

2.4.5.2 Deemed 21-Year Disposition Rule

The *Income Tax Act* requires most personal trusts are deemed to dispose of their property once every 21 years. Otherwise, a trust could accumulate property for generations without paying tax. Ordinarily, prior to the 21 years, the trust can be wound up on a tax-deferred basis if certain conditions exist. Consult your Chartered Accountant.

2.4.5.3 Preferred Beneficiary Election

A preferred beneficiary election is a provision under the *Income Tax Act* which permits income that is earned and accumulated in an *inter vivos* trust to be reported in the beneficiary's income for the year, which can result in significant tax savings. An *inter vivos* trust is taxed on its income at the highest marginal rate, currently 29%. An individual is taxed on their income at the graduated tax rates which range from 15%, 22%, 26% to 29% federally, plus provincial taxes, depending on the amount of income being reported by the individual. If the individual is in the lowest tax bracket, the income reported by the *inter vivos* trust will be taxed at 15% instead of 29% federally plus provincial taxes.

A preferred beneficiary must be eligible for the disability tax credit and may be any of the settlor, the settlor's former or current spouse/common-law partner, a child, grandchild or great grandchild.

An election must be filed for each tax year that the election applies. The election must include a statement that makes the election for a specific taxation year, must designate the accumulating income that is the subject of the election, must state that the trustee and beneficiary are authorized to make the election and must be signed by both the trustee and preferred beneficiary. A statement must also be included that shows how the preferred beneficiary's share of the accumulating income is calculated. The calculation must be in accordance with the *Act*. Other information regarding the applicable trust provisions and their administration must also be included.

2.4.5.4 Spousal Trusts and Similar Trusts

The *Income Tax Act* provides for individuals to transfer property to certain trusts on a tax-deferred basis if prescribed conditions are met. These trusts include a spousal/common-law partner trust, joint spousal/common-law partner trust, alter-ego trust and self-interest trust.

These trusts may be used for several purposes such as for asset protection, estate freezes or to pass property outside of the estate. Property that is passed outside of the estate is not subject to probate fees/tax. These trusts can also hold the principal residence if conditions set out in the *Income Tax Act* are met.

These trusts are all personal trusts and will not meet the criteria required for each type of trust if consideration is received. The rollover will also be denied where there is reasonable belief that the transferor is about to emigrate and become a non-resident. A person is deemed to dispose of all of their property when they become a non-resident and that property becomes subject to tax on capital gains.

> A spousal or alter-ego trust can help avoid probate

2.4.5.5 Spousal/Common-Law Partner Trust

A spousal/common-law partner trust is created by a spouse/common-law partner either during their life or upon their death. The creator or settlor can transfer property into the trust on a tax-deferred (rollover) basis if no consideration is received. A spousal/common-law partner trust can entitle only the beneficiary spouse/common-law partner to receive the income of the trust that arises before their death and only the beneficiary spouse may receive or have use of any income or capital of the trust before their death. In the case of a testamentary trust, the trust property must vest in the trust within 36 months of its creation. There are also Canadian residency requirements to be met. Consult your Chartered Accountant and lawyer to ensure that this type of trust is properly created and maintained.

2.4.5.6 Joint Spouse/Common-Law Partner Trusts

A joint spouse/common-law partner trust is created by an individual, while alive, who is at least 65 years old. The creator or settlor can transfer property into the trust on a tax-deferred (rollover) basis if no consideration is received. The individual who created the trust and their spouse/common-law partner are the only designated beneficiaries and are the only ones entitled to receive any of the trust capital or any income that the trust earns during their lifetimes. No other person is entitled to any of the capital or income of the trust before the later of the spouses dies. The 21-year deemed disposition rule does not apply during the lifetimes of the spouses/common-law partners. There is a deemed disposition at fair market value on the death of the later spouse and every 21 years thereafter.

2.4.5.7 Alter-Ego Trusts

An alter-ego trust is created by an individual, while alive, who is at least 65 years old. The creator or settlor can transfer property into the trust on a tax deferred (rollover) basis if no consideration is received. The individual is the designated beneficiary and is the only beneficiary entitled to receive any of the income earned by, or capital of, the trust during the individual's lifetime. The 21-year deemed disposition rule does not apply during the individual's lifetime. There is a deemed disposition at fair market value on the death of the individual and every 21 years thereafter.

2.4.5.8 Self-Benefit Trust

A self-benefit trust is created by an individual while they are alive. There is no age restriction. The creator or settlor can transfer property into the trust on a tax-deferred (rollover) basis if no consideration is received. The individual who created the trust must be the only beneficiary entitled to receive all of the trust capital and all of the income that the trust earns during their lifetime. Another person or partnership cannot have any absolute or contingent beneficial interest in the trust. The 21-year deemed disposition rule at fair market value applies during the individual's lifetime.

2.5 BUSINESS SUCCESSION

If you own a business, it is important to give some thought to who will inherit and run it after your death.

Your choice of estate-planning tools used to transfer a business will often depend on whether you plan to retire from the business or keep it until your death. Business succession planning generally considers both the continuity of the business and the minimization of adverse tax consequences. As part of the process, you should consult a Chartered Accountant and an estate-planning lawyer.

Here are some questions to ask yourself:
- Who do you want to succeed you in your business? (This could be a family member, employee, an unknown and unrelated third party buyer, or you may consider that merging with a competitor would be the best option.)
- Do you want the transition to be immediate or would you like to stay involved and have your participation reduced over time?
- Who will train the successor and what will their training period look like?
- Who else is involved in the transition? Are there other managers or employees to consider?
- How will ownership be transferred: to one other owner or several?
- Do you want an asset sale or a share sale?
- What is the value of the assets?
- What is the value of the shares?

- What are the tax and legal implications?
- Are there other financial implications?
- How will the process be monitored?
- What is the timetable for the transition? What does the timeline look like?
- How will disputes be handled?

Selling a business can be more than just the dollars and cents, particularly if you have a family business. There may be emotional ties to the business and each family member may have a different relationship to the business, such as wanting or being active in the business or not wanting anything to do with business operations at all. Consider the perspectives of all involved: yourself, your spouse/partner, your children, and other key people that are affected by this situation. A family business advisor can help you deal with family disputes and emotional issues that may arise. See the Resources section for contact information.

2.5.1 ESTATE FREEZES

Chartered Accountants use the term "estate freeze" to define transactions where an asset of growing value is exchanged for an asset of fixed value. A common example would be where a business owner transfers their common shares that they own in their operating company to a holding company for special shares. Family members and sometimes a family trust will subscribe for the common shares of the holding company. In this way, the growth of the operating company is passed on to other family members. Professional advice is recommended. An estate plan gone wrong could inadvertently attract the anti-avoidance provisions under the *Income Tax Act*, such as the attribution rules or the general anti-avoidance rule, if not properly executed.

2.5.2 DOCUMENTS

It is important to collect all your documents involving your business. A prudent investor would conduct a due diligence review prior to buying a business. You should be familiar with the elements of a due diligence review which can help you make sure your business is ready for the transition.

Documents for due diligence include:
- organizational chart of the company including all subsidiary companies
- constating documents, such as articles of incorporation or partnership agreement

- list of all jurisdictions where the business operates
- applicable legislation
- articles, by-laws, minute books in the case of a corporation, partnership agreement, business registration or other constating document
- shareholder agreements
- compliance with all regulatory and industry requirements
- loan documents and liens
- ownership and title history of assets
- financial statements and related documents
- deeds of real property and any outstanding issues such as environmental assessments
- insurance
- all contracts involving the business
- employment, independent contractor and union contracts, and related documents
- pending or ongoing litigation documents
- documentation involving environmental matters
- transactions involving related parties
- intellectual property rights, contracts, licences, trade-marks, copyrights, patents and related matters
- other documents particular to your business or industry.

Consult your professional advisors to discuss the options available to you for business succession.

In corporations where the shares are held by few shareholders, it is the interest of the shareholders that should be served. A unanimous shareholders agreement (USA) allows shareholders to choose the corporation's control and management structure. USAs may provide for a restriction on the transfer of shares. The shares of a corporation are less marketable if a USA is in effect. The USA usually provides a method for the shareholder to sell shares or for new shareholders to buy shares. An example of this is a "buy-sell" clause. This allows an existing shareholder to keep control of their interest in a business until a triggering event occurs, such as retirement, divorce, disability, or death. When the triggering event occurs, the buyer is obligated to buy the shareholder's interest at the fair market value. The buyer can be a person, a group (such as co-owners), or the business itself. Price and sale terms are prearranged, which eliminates the need for a fire sale if you become ill or die.

2.6 CAPITAL GAINS EXEMPTIONS

Generally, capital property is taxed at 50% on the capital gains that are realized on disposition of the property. The *Income Tax Act* provides some exemptions as noted below. See also Section 1.3 for a discussion on the principal residence exemption.

2.6.1 $100,000 CAPITAL GAINS EXEMPTION (REPEALED FEBRUARY 23, 1994)

Prior to February 23, 1994, a $100,000 lifetime capital gains exemption was available on the disposition of capital property, for example, a cottage. An election was available at the time of repealing the provision for taxpayers to trigger the capital gains exemption to increase the adjusted cost base of the property for the time of disposition.

2.6.2 LIFETIME CAPITAL GAINS DEDUCTION

A $750,000 lifetime capital gains deduction is available when you dispose of qualified farm property, qualified fishing property and qualified small business shares. The lifetime limit was increased from $500,000 as of March 19, 2007. Dispositions of qualified fishing property have been included since May 2, 2006.

2.6.2.1 Qualified Small Business Corporation Shares

The following conditions must be met:
- the shares are owned by yourself, a related person or your partnership at least 24 months before the sale
- the shares are of a corporation that is a Canadian-controlled private corporation and substantially all assets (90% of the fair market value of its assets) are used primarily in an active business in Canada
- the shareholder must have acquired the shares from an unrelated party at least 24 months (holding period) prior to the sale, and
- during the holding period, at least 50% of the fair market value of the assets must have been used carrying on an active business in Canada.

2.6.2.2 Qualified Farm Property

Qualified farm property is, for a minimum of 24 months immediately prior to disposition, owned by you, your spouse/common-law partner or partnership and is used by you, your spouse/common-law partner, child, parent, personal trust, or

partnership with an interest in your or your spouse's/common-law partner's family farm partnership. The property can be real or immovable property that is used principally in the business of farming in Canada. Draft legislation announced on November 5, 2010 will remove the word "principally" for dispositions on or after May 1, 2006.

The property will qualify if, during a minimum of two years while the property was owned by one or more of the above-named persons, either:

- the gross income from farming of one of the owners who is operating the farm exceeds their income from all other sources for at least two years, and
- the property has been principally used in the farming business in Canada by an owner, or the beneficiary where the property is owned by a personal trust, who was continuously and regularly involved in the business

  or:

- the farm has been operated for at least 24 months by an owner who was continuously and regularly involved in the farming business in Canada and the property is used by a corporation or a partnership.

If you own farmland and buildings that were acquired on or before June 17, 1987 and they are used in a farming business by yourself, your spouse/common-law partner, parent or child, your property will qualify if the farming business was carried out either for at least five years during the time that you owned the property or during the year that you dispose of the property.

2.6.2.3 Qualified Fishing Property

Qualified fishing property includes fishing vessels, and real or immovable property that is owned by you, your spouse/common-law or partnership and is used principally in a fishing business in Canada by you, your spouse/common-law partner, child, parent, family fishing corporation or partnership, personal trust or trust beneficiary. Draft legislation announced on November 5, 2010 will remove the word "principally" for dispositions on or after May 1, 2006.

In order for the property to be qualified fishing property for the purpose of using the lifetime capital gains exemption, the property must:

- be used by you, your spouse/common-law partner, child, parent, family fishing partnership or personal trust at least 24 months immediately prior to the sale, and

- have a gross income that exceeds the income from all other sources of one of the persons named above who is operating the business for at least two years, and have been either principally used in the fishing business, or the beneficiary of a personal trust was continuously and regularly involved in the business, or

- has been used by a corporation or partnership for at least 24 months in the fishing business in which an eligible individual has been continuously and regularly involved in the business.

2.6.3 PRINCIPAL RESIDENCE EXEMPTION

If you have lived in your home since you bought it, any capital gains realized when you sell your house will be tax exempt if certain conditions set out in the *Income Tax Act* are met. Only one principal residence may be designated in a year. A prescribed form must be filed in situations where there are capital gains to report. Consult your Chartered Accountant.

2.7 **CHARITABLE DONATIONS**

The eligible amount of donations up to $200 that are made by an individual taxpayer during the year to a registered charity can be claimed for a tax credit at the lowest marginal tax rate (15%). The eligible amount of donations that is over $200 can be claimed for a tax credit at the highest marginal tax rate (29%). A taxpayer can donate up to 75% of their net income in a year. Excess amounts can be carried forward for five years. The eligible amount is a draft provision that clarifies the amount used to claim the tax credit is the fair market value that exceeds any advantage that the taxpayer may have received. Where an advantage exceeds 80% of the fair market value of the gift, a request must be made to the Minister of Revenue to approve that a gift is intended before a tax credit can be claimed. The 75% is increased to 100% in the year of death and the year preceding death. There are special tax rules for donations of property such as cultural property, ecologically sensitive land and certain company shares.

A corporation can also donate up to 75% of its net income annually to registered charities and receive a tax deduction for the donated amount. Excess donations can be carried forward five years.

There are exceptions to the 75% rule when certain property is donated such as cultural property, ecologically sensitive land, and certain securities. Specific requirements of the *Income Tax Act* must be met and may form part of your succession plan. Professional advice is recommended to determine the proper structure for you.

2.7.1 CULTURAL PROPERTY

Cultural property must be assessed at fair market value by the Canadian Cultural Property Export Review Board which is good for two years from the date of determination. Donated cultural property is tax exempt from capital gains tax to the donor. Institutions are required to keep cultural property they receive as donations for 10 years.

2.7.2 ECOLOGICALLY SENSITIVE LAND

Donations of ecologically sensitive land must be certified by the Minister of Environment under the Ecological Gifts Program in order for the donor to receive the capital gains tax rate of 0%. The land may be donated to a registered charitable organization or registered public foundation. The Minister of Environment will certify the fair market value of the gift, which is valid for two years.

2.7.3 DONATIONS OF PUBLICLY TRADED SECURITIES

Donations of certain publicly traded securities to registered charities, public foundations and private foundations are taxed at the preferred capital gains tax rate of 0%. Donations of the proceeds of the same securities had they been sold prior to donation would be taxed at the capital gains rate of 50%. Special anti-avoidance provisions apply to the donations of shares to private foundations. Employees who donate shares that they have acquired through a stock option within 30 days of the acquisition may also qualify for the preferred capital gains tax rate of 0%. Professional advice is recommended.

2.8 FUNERAL WISHES

Specifics of a funeral service and whether to be buried or cremated are personal decisions. Reflect on your own beliefs and discuss your choices with your loved ones. Be sure to tell them if you have prepaid for anything and where related documents are stored. Write down your wishes and give copies to your family and your lawyer.

Each province and territory has laws regulating funeral services, burial, and cremation. For example, embalming is not generally required by law in most situations. It may, however, be required when transporting a body out of province or country or when using a common carrier. In some jurisdictions, a funeral home will usually embalm a body unless instructed otherwise. Further information can be obtained from the applicable consumer affairs office. See Canada's Office of Consumer Affairs for regional consumer affairs offices at **www.ic.gc.ca/eic/site/ic1.nsf/eng/h_00021.html.**

> **Best planning tool—tell people what you want**

While it may be uncomfortable to talk about, discussing wishes for funeral services and burial or cremation can bring comfort to family members in a time of grief.

2.8.1 VETERAN AFFAIRS: THE LAST POST FUND

Let your family know if you are a veteran who would qualify for The Last Post Fund. Funeral and burial assistance is available when a Veteran dies as a result of an awarded or pensioned disability. Assistance is also available for Veterans who have insufficient funds in their estate. A military style grave marker can also be provided as part of assisted services. A request for assisted service must be made within one year of the Veteran's death. More information is available by calling 1-800-465-7113 or online at **www.lastpostfund.ca/**.

CHAPTER 3
SURVIVOR ISSUES

The issues of tracking assets and liabilities, adjusting to altered sources of revenue, care of dependants, managing financial affairs, and accessing available resources and benefits may shift, after death, to one or more loved ones. This booklet contains the framework and structure to accomplish this shift. Surviving family members are frequently thrust into new and unfamiliar roles in managing finances as family members and loved ones seek information, reassurance and security in the months and years after a death.

Some of the issues related to financial affairs facing survivors are immediate or short-term, while others may arise months or even a year or more after a family member's death. The following suggestions are meant only as guidelines to help the bereaved set some priorities when the number of required tasks may seem overwhelming.

The bereaved should avoid:
- thinking about moving from their current home until they can make a decision that is based on reason and not emotion
- spending money impulsively
- caving into pressure to sell or give away the deceased's possessions
- giving or lending money to others without reviewing finances first.

3.1 OTHER CONSIDERATIONS

Depending on the family dynamics and specifics of the situation, professionals often recommend that major financial changes and decisions be delayed for six to 12 months following the death of a loved one. Although this may not always be practical, you should consider that highly emotional times could skew your ability to make good financial decisions. Survivors, for example, may feel the need to rush to pay all outstanding bills immediately. It should be noted that survivors are not responsible for the individual debts of the deceased. Consequently, personal assets of the survivor and the estate should not be mixed.

When you post an obituary, you are giving public notice not only that someone has died, but also when services will be held. Unfortunately, this can provide an opportunity for criminals to approach survivors and indicate that goods or services have been purchased and payment is due. Publication of the date and time of the funeral service may also be an invitation for criminals to rob the empty home of the deceased. Steps should be taken to secure the premises adequately and avoid fraudulent transactions.

> Carefully consider major decisions during highly emotional times

3.1.1 CANADA PENSION PLAN SURVIVOR BENEFITS

CPP survivor benefits are paid to the deceased contributor's surviving spouse (common law partner) and dependant children. There are three types of benefits:

1. **Death Benefit:** one-time payment to the estate of the deceased's Canada Pension Plan contribution.

2. **Survivor's Pension:** monthly pension paid to the surviving spouse (common law partner) of the deceased contributor.

3. **Child's Benefit:** monthly benefit for dependent children of the deceased contributor.

The death benefit is a maximum of $2,500 or six months worth of calculated retirement pension if the deceased had been age 65 when death occurred. The benefit is taxable to the recipient, either the estate or the beneficiary. To qualify, the minimum contribution period must be met.

The survivor's benefit is determined by the amount that the deceased would have received if they had been 65 at the time of death and also the age of the survivor. See the Service Canada Website for current rates: **www.servicecanada.gc.ca**.

The child's benefit is available for a child who has lost at least one parent who was a resident CPP contributor. The taxable monthly child's benefit is a flat rate and is adjusted annually. An application in writing must be made. If the application is made late, the benefits can start up to 11 months prior to the month of application but no sooner than the month after the contributor's death. If the child is under the age of 18, the benefit is generally paid to the person with whom the person is living.

After application survivor benefits normally take six to 12 weeks for the first payment to be made. Back payments can be made for up to 12 months in the event that there is a delay in applying.

CHAPTER 4
PERSONAL REPRESENTATIVE RESPONSIBILITIES

4.1 INCOME TAX RETURN FILING OBLIGATIONS

4.1.1 TERMINAL RETURN

For deaths that occur on or after January 1 to October 31 in a taxation year, the filing date for the terminal return is April 30 of the following year.

For deaths that occur on or after November 1 to December 31 in a taxation year, the filing date for the terminal return is six months following the date of death.

This filing deadline applies for the spouse/common-law partner of the deceased although any taxes owing are due on April 30.

Where the deceased or their spouse/common-law partner were carrying on a business at the time of death, the filing deadline is June 15 for deaths occurring on or after January 1 to December 15 and six months after the date of death for deaths occurring on or after December 16 to December 31.

4.1.2 DECEASED'S PREVIOUS YEAR TAX RETURN

Where a deceased dies before filing the previous year's tax return, the deadline to file that return is six months after the date of death. For example a person who dies in January of a taxation year has probably not filed their return for the previous year, which would normally be due April 30. Rather than being due April 30, it is due six months after the date of death.

Where the will or a court order establishes a testamentary spousal or common-law partner trust and testamentary debts are being paid by the trust, the due date for the final return is extended to 18 months following the date of death, although taxes remain owing by the due date.

4.1.3 RIGHTS AND THINGS RETURN

Amounts that have not yet been paid to the deceased at the time of death that would have been paid and included in their return if they were still alive can be included on the Rights and Things Return.

Rights and things include:
- amounts owed by the employer at the date of death
- amounts owed by the employer for a pay period that was completed prior to the date of death
- Old Age Security benefits
- bond coupons that have matured but have not been cashed
- unpaid and unreported bond interest that was earned before the date of death
- unpaid dividends that were declared prior to the date of death
- where the deceased was a farmer or fisherman who used the cash method, any accounts receivable, inventory and supplies on hand
- where the deceased used the cash method, livestock that is not part of the herd and harvested farm crops
- work in progress, where the deceased was a professional sole proprietor and had elected to exclude work in progress when calculating their income. A professional who can elect to exclude work in progress includes accountants, chiropractors, dentists, lawyers, advocates or notaries in Quebec, medical doctors, and veterinarians.

A rights and things return is filed by using a T1 General Income Tax and Benefit Return with "70(2)" written at the top of the return. This return must be filed by the later of one year after the date of death or 90 days after the CRA mails the notice of assessment or reassessment of the final return. However, the due date to pay any balance owing is April 30 of the year following death where the death occurs on or after January 1 to October 31, or six months after the date of the death when the death occurs on or after November 1 to December 31, unless an election is filed in prescribed form to pay later. Interest will still be charged for any amounts owing after the due date.

4.1.4 RETURN OF A PARTNER OR PROPRIETOR

If the deceased had a fiscal period that is different from the calendar taxation year, an optional return can be filed. Income reported on this return is for the period after the fiscal period of the last return and the date of death. This return is filed by using a T1 General Income Tax and Benefit Return and writing "150(4)" at the top of the return. The filing deadline and due date deadline for taxes owing are the same as the final return.

4.1.5 TESTAMENTARY TRUST RETURN

A testamentary trust return is filed by using a T3 Trust Income Tax and Information Return. This return must be filed and taxes are due the same as the final return.

You can claim some of the personal tax credits on each of the final return and optional returns including:
- the basic personal amount
- age amount
- spouse/common-law partner amount
- eligible dependant amount
- infirm dependants age 18 or older amount
- caregiver amount.

Other amounts can be split between the returns including as an example,
- the disability amount for the deceased, and the disability amount that is transferred from a dependant
- charitable donations that do not exceed the net income reported on that return
- cultural, ecological and Crown gifts
- home buyers' amount.

4.2 TIMELINE AND CHECKLIST OF TASKS

The executor of a will has many tasks to complete in administering and settling an estate. Obtain professional advice when necessary.

A lawyer can interpret the will, advise the executor of their duties, identify legal issues, advise on whether or not probate is required, represent the executor in court, prepare legal documents regarding transferring or selling the estate assets, and prepare releases for the beneficiaries.

4.2.1 IMMEDIATELY AFTER DEATH CHECKLIST

☐	Arrange for organ donation where applicable
☐	Arrange for care of minors
☐	Arrange for care of pets
☐	Obtain death certificate or statement of death from the funeral director and get several original copies
☐	Arrange for or assist with funeral service and burial or cremation
☐	Arrange to take care of perishable food, plants and disposables
☐	Locate the original Last Will and Testament of the deceased
☐	Go to the safe deposit box
☐	Arrange for security of the decedent's home, car, motor home, property or business, other valuable assets and review that adequate insurance is in place
☐	Contact the post office to arrange for mail delivery of the deceased to be redirected to the executor (Canada Post will waive the change of address fee if proper documentation is provided)
☐	Notify the CRA of the deceased's date of death and provide them with death certificate and will or letters of probate
☐	Consider appointing a legal representative to deal with the CRA with respect to the estate
☐	Open account for the deceased's estate
☐	Cancel credit cards on which the deceased was the only signer and return the cards to issuers or destroy them
☐	Notify all other credit card companies where deceased had an account with another person

4.2.2 INTERIM CHECKLIST

☐	Locate all important documents
☐	Locate and prepare a list of assets that are owned by the deceased
☐	Prepare a list of legitimate debts of the deceased
☐	Locate and notify beneficiaries, confirm contact and any other applicable information and discuss the process of administering the will
☐	Get valuations of real property and other valuable assets where required
☐	Consider consulting with a lawyer to discuss the estate, any potential contentious claims, liabilities, debts and other legal issues
☐	Apply for probate if required and pay applicable probate fees (valuation of estate is required to determine probate fees/taxes)
☐	Notify and Request death benefits from Canada Pension Plan, OAS, other pensions, life insurance policies and annuities
☐	Advertise for creditors
☐	Consult a lawyer before requesting distribution of retirement benefits
☐	Cancel newspapers, subscriptions and other home deliveries and request refunds where applicable
☐	Pick up personal effects from the long-term care home
☐	Notify Service Canada, Passport Canada, provincial health ministry and other government agencies where applicable
☐	Finish gathering and organizing financial documents
☐	If a trust is involved, consult a lawyer
☐	Evaluate business and partnership obligations. If necessary, notify the decedent's employer or other business contacts. Collect information on the disposition of the deceased's last paycheque, company life insurance, pension benefits, money in deferred compensation or profit-sharing accounts
☐	Pay funeral expenses, taxes and legitimate debts

4.2.3 FINAL MATTERS CHECKLIST

☐	Subject to the will and investment powers: • convert assets into cash • deposit in estate account • invest
☐	Prepare outstanding tax returns including any outstanding prior year return: • Terminal T-1 Return • T-3 Trust and Estate Return and, where applicable: • a partnership stub return (for the period from the beginning of the tax year to the date of death) • trust stub return (for the period from the beginning of the tax year to the date of death), and • a rights and things return
☐	Request a Clearance Certificate from the Canada Revenue Agency that indicates all outstanding tax liabilities have been paid
☐	Deliver personal property, in accordance with the will, to the beneficiaries
☐	Prepare an account showing: • original assets • income receipts • capital receipts • income disbursements • capital disbursements • compensation
☐	Obtain signed release from beneficiaries
☐	Distribute estate to beneficiaries and notify them of any tax liability
☐	Close the estate account

4.3 GST/HST CREDIT AND OTHER BENEFITS

Arrange to have payments stopped or transferred to a survivor, if applicable, in any of the following situations where the deceased was receiving:

- the GST/HST credit
- the working income tax benefit (WITB) advance payments
- benefit payments for a child — Canada Child Tax Benefit (CCTB) and/or Universal Child Care Benefit (UCCB), or where CCTB and/or GST/HST and/or UCCB payments are made for the deceased who was a child.

Do not pay instalment payments that are due after the deceased's death. Pay any outstanding instalment payments that were due prior to the deceased's death.

Return any GST/HST payment that is sent out after the deceased's death. GST/HST credits are generally issued on the fifth day of each of July, October, January and April and may be issued prior to the CRA being made aware of the deceased's death. If the deceased died before a schedule month of issue, no more payments will be made to that person or to their estate. Where the deceased died during or after the scheduled month of issue and the payment has not been cashed, return the cheque to the CRA so that they can issue the payment to the deceased's estate.

Where the deceased was receiving a credit for a child, inform the new caregiver to request payments from the CRA for the child.

The deceased's spouse or common-law partner may qualify to receive the GST/HST credit payments based on their income alone.

The deceased's spouse or common-law partner should contact the CRA if the deceased's GST/HST credit included them and any children and should file an Income Tax and Benefit Return, as applicable, for prior years if not already done.

A person receiving a GST/HST credit for a child who has died should contact the CRA as soon as possible with the date of death.

4.4 UNCLAIMED FUNDS

The deceased's personal representative can contact their local tax services office to determine whether there is an unclaimed tax refund. Canadian banks are required to try to contact owners of bank accounts with unclaimed balances of $10 or more following each of the second and fifth years of inactivity and to publish notices in the *Canada Gazette*. Banks are required to hold account balances for ten years from the last bank transaction by the account owner. The Bank of Canada is required to hold accounts worth less than $1,000 for a further thirty years. The Bank of Canada is required to hold unclaimed accounts worth $1,000 or more indefinitely until the account is claimed. The Bank of Canada maintains a database of unclaimed balances. See **ucbswww.bank-banque-canada.ca/scripts/search_english.cfm**

CHAPTER 5
GATHERING AND ORGANIZING

At any stage in life, it is important to have easy access to important documents. For example, for your own planning and decision-making purposes, you'll want to be able to easily determine your assets (what you own) and your liabilities (what you owe). You will also need to know where key papers and documents are located. Once you have the documents you need, it is a good idea to store them all but legal directives discussed in Section 1.1 in a safe deposit box or fireproof home safe.

> **Are your documents up-to-date?**
>
> **Can you quickly locate them in an emergency?**

5.1 CHECKLIST OF DOCUMENTS

This list of documents have been discussed in this *Guide* and may be required by an executor. Documents that are not applicable can be marked with N/A.

DOCUMENT TYPE	SECTION	
Advance directive	1.1.1	
Assets held in trusts	2.3.3	
Auto and home insurance agents	4.2	
Bank accounts	4.2	
Bank books and statements	4.2	
Banker	4.2	
Beneficiary designations for RRIFs, RRSPs, RSPs, TFSAs, life insurance, annuities, other	4.2	
Birth certificate	4.2	
Business registration	2.5.2, 4.2	
Business documents	2.4.2	
Canada Pension Plan/Quebec Pension Plan	1.2.7	
Capital gains elections	1.3, 2.6	
Caregiver expenses	1.4.2	
Charitable donations	2.6	
Chartered accountant	4.2	
Choice of guardian(s) for children	2.2.5, 4.2	
Constating document	2.5.2	
Credit card statements	4.2	
Death certificate	4.2	
Deeds and titles to real and personal property, including cars, motor-cycles, boats and airplanes	4.2	
Disability Certificate	1.4.5	
Disability insurance	1.2.1	
Disability supports expenses	1.4.1	
Divorce decrees	4.2	

DOCUMENT TYPE	SECTION	
Do Not Resuscitate (DNR) order	1.1.5	
Employee benefits	4.2	
Employment history	1.2.6, 4.2	
Executor	4.2	
Extended Health Care	1.1.3	
Family members	4.2	
Financial planner	4.2	
Funeral wishes, prepayments	2.8 , 4.2	
General partnership agreement	2.5.2, 4.2	
House deed	1.3, 4.2	
Incorporation documents	2.5.2, 4.2	
Insurance policies	4.2	
Intellectual property rights	2.5.2	
Investment statements (mutual funds, RRSPs, RRIFs, RSPs, TFSAs, brokerage)	4.2	
Last will and testament	2.2, 4.2	
Latest financial statements (personal or business)	4.2	
Lawyer	4.2	
Life Insurance	2.2.5, 2.4, 2.4.4, 4.2	
Life, health, long-term care and disability insurance policies	4.2	
Limited liability partnership agreement	2.5.2, 4.2	
Limited partnership agreement	2.5.2, 4.2	
List of appointments as trustee or guardian	4.2	
List of assets jointly owned with spouse	2.3, 4.2	
List of assets wholly owned	4.2	
List of beneficiaries	2.2.5	
List of family property	2.3.2	
Living will	1.1.2	
Loan documents	2.5.2, 4.2	

DOCUMENT TYPE	SECTION	
Long-term Care Insurance	1.2.5	
Marriage certificate	4.2	
Medical expenses	1.4.4	
Membership cards	4.2	
Military records	4.2	
Mortgage	1.3, 1.3.1, 4.2	
Other housing documents	1.3, 4.2	
Ownership and history of assets	2.5.2	
Passport	4.2	
Pensions	4.2	
Power of attorney for personal care/Health care proxy	1.1.2	
Power of attorney for property	1.1.4	
Principal Residence Exemption	2.6.3	
Probate	2.2.3	
Pre-nuptial and other domestic agreements	4.2	
Records and documents • for at least six years if you filed on time; • six years since a return was filed if later; or • for longer periods in certain circumstances	4.2	
Registered Disability Savings Plan	2.4.3	
Registered Retirement Income Fund	1.2.11	
Registered Retirement Savings Plan	1.2.10	
Related business documents	2.5.2, 4.2	
Retirement benefits	4.2	
Retirement pensions and income funds	1.2.6, 4.2	
Safe deposit boxes	4.2	
Shareholder or Unanimous Shareholder Agreement	2.4.2, 4.2	
Tax-free Savings Account	1.2.12	
Tax returns from the last six years	4.2	
Terminal and other tax returns	4.1, 4.2	

DOCUMENT TYPE	SECTION	
Testamentary wills (include multiple wills)	2.2, 4.2	
Trust Instruments	2.4.5, 4.2	
U.S. Social Security Benefits	1.2.14	
Valuation Reports	2.5.2	

Knowing in advance where these documents are kept will serve to reduce the stress of locating them at a time when your attention is needed in other areas.

There may be other documents that are not financial in matter, but will give peace of mind—for instance, where the septic tank is buried.

CHAPTER 6
RESOURCES

The material contained in this booklet is designed to introduce some basic and fundamental topics related to managing financial affairs during and at the end of life. These topics can be fairly dense and complex. Information about resources and referral centres for Chartered Accountants, lawyers, financial planners and government agencies are provided below.

CHARTERED ACCOUNTANT (CA)

CAs can assist individuals with a variety of financial issues, including tax and financial planning, management consulting and business valuation. In addition, PrimePlus/ElderCare services aim to integrate these planning strategies with the care goals of family members when elderly family members are no longer able to act independently.

www.cica.ca

www.cica.ca/primeplus

LAWYER

A lawyer can assist individuals with a variety of legal issues, including wills, estates, trusts and healthcare advance planning. Individuals are advised to seek the advice of an experienced lawyer when dealing with any identified legal issue.

The Federation of Law Societies of Canada co-ordinates the 14 law societies across Canada. Their website has links to each law society as well as affiliated bodies, such as the Canadian Bar Association. The Federation administers the search engine CanLII (**www.canlii.org**) which provides free public access to the laws and court decisions in Canada.

www.flsc.ca/en/about/about.asp

CANADIAN BAR ASSOCIATION — NATIONAL ELDER LAW SECTION

www.cba.org/cba/sections_elder/main/

TRUST AND ESTATE PRACTITIONERS

THE SOCIETY OF TRUST AND ESTATE PRACTITIONERS

The Society of Trust and Estate Practitioners (STEP Canada) has over 2,000 members in Canada. This multi-disciplinary organization has experienced and senior practitioners, including Chartered Accountants, financial planners, insurance advisors, lawyers, and trust professionals. There are branch offices in the Atlantic region, Calgary, Edmonton, Montreal, Ottawa, Toronto, Vancouver and Winnipeg.

www.step.ca

FINANCIAL PLANNERS

FINANCIAL PLANNING STANDARDS COUNCIL

The Financial Planning Standards Council (FPSC) is a not-for-profit organization that develops, promotes and enforces professional standards for financial planners through a certification process. Their website hosts a searchable financial planner database.

www.fpsc.ca/directory-cfp-professionals-good-standing

ADVOCIS THE FINANCIAL ADVISORS ASSOCIATION OF CANADA

This voluntary membership association of professional financial advisors in Canada has over 10,000 members and 43 chapters across Canada. The link below offers descriptions of the different designations of financial advisors including Chartered Accountants, Chartered Life Underwriters (CLU) (specialists in estate planning and life insurance), Registered Health Underwriters (specialists in living benefits) and Elder Planning Counselors (EPC) (specialists with an understanding of the specific issues of aging).

www.advocis.ca/content/consumers/designations.html

THE CANADIAN LIFE AND HEALTH INSURANCE ASSOCIATION

The Canadian Life and Health Insurance Association is a voluntary trade association comprised of life and health insurers in Canada.

www.clhia.ca

SUCCESSION PLANNING CONSULTANTS/FAMILY BUSINESS FACILITATORS

CANADIAN ASSOCIATION OF FAMILY ENTERPRISES (CAFE)

CAFE provides a registry of Family Business Advisors.

www.cafenational.org/

THE BUSINESS FAMILIES FOUNDATION

This Foundation has family business centres at the University of British Columbia, University of Alberta, McGill University and Dalhousie University.

www.famillesenaffaires.com

GOVERNMENT AND OTHER RESOURCES

BIRTH, MARRIAGE AND DEATH CERTIFICATES

These certificates can be obtained from the provincial registry (often called Vital Statistics). Contact information is available through Canada Online at **canadaonline.about.com/od/vitalstatistics/Vital_Statistics_Offices_in_Canada.htm**

CANADA BENEFITS

Information about federal and provincial programs for seniors including Canada Pensions Plan and Old Age Security is provided here:

www.canadabenefits.gc.ca/faechome.jsp?lang=en

CANADA REVENUE AGENCY

www.cra-arc.gc.ca

CANADIAN HEALTHCARE ASSOCIATION

www.cha.ca/

CANADIAN HOSPICE PALLIATIVE CARE ASSOCIATION

www.chpca.net

CANADIAN MEDICAL ASSOCIATION

www.cma.ca

CANADIAN MENTAL HEALTH ASSOCIATION

www.cmha.ca

CPP/QPP GOVERNMENT PROGRAM PAYMENTS

CPP/QPP administer different benefit programs for which you or a family member may be eligible. For current, average and maximum amounts of the different types of benefits, see **www.servicecanada.gc.ca/eng/isp/pub/factsheets/rates.shtml**.

FINANCIAL CONSUMER AGENCY OF CANADA (FCAC)

www.fcac-acfc.gc.ca/

HEALTH INSURANCE IN CANADA

Provides information on private health care insurance and has links to each provincial and territorial health plan summary and the applicable health care ministry.

www.healthinsurancecanada.com/

LONG-TERM CARE INSURANCE

www.longtermcarecanada.com

OFFICE OF CONSUMER AFFAIRS INDUSTRY CANADA

www.consumer.ic.gc.ca/

PERSONS WITH DISABILITIES ONLINE

www.pwd-online.ca

SENIORS CANADA

www.seniors.gc.ca

SERVICE CANADA

This government portal provides one-stop access to delivery of many government programs including: the Canada Pension Plan, Home Adaptations for Seniors Program from CMHC, and passport services.

www.servicecanada.gc.ca/en/home.shtml

TAXATION FOR SENIORS

Information on filing tax returns, Registered Retirement Savings Plan, Attendant Care Expenses Paid to a Retirement Home and more.

www.cra-arc.gc.ca/seniors/

CHAPTER 7
GLOSSARY

Advance Directives

   Legal document written by an attorney or the person directing the physician about a patient's request for terminal care; can designate whom a patient selects for making medical decisions when the patient is no longer able to do so.

Amendment

   Any change (addition or deletion) in a legal document.

Ancillary

   Something that is subordinate or auxiliary to something or someone else.

Annuitant

   The beneficiary of an annuity.

Annuity

   The payment of an allowance or income, either annually or at other intervals, for a lifetime or for a certain number of years.

Attorney (Agent)

A person who holds a power of attorney that has written authorization to transact business and execute documents for another person.

Beneficiary

The person who collects the benefits from a will, trust or pension.

Bequest

An act of giving a gift of personal property by will.

Codicil

A supplement or appendix to a will; intended to alter an already executed will.

Community Property or Family Property

Classification of property equally owned by a husband and wife that was acquired during their marriage.

Constructive Trust

Without regarding the intention of the parties, this trust is created by a court as a means of justice to benefit the party that has been mistakenly deprived of its rights.

Contest of a Will

A legal process attempting to prevent the probate of a will or the distribution of property according to the will.

Corporate Fiduciary

A bank or trust institution with fiduciary powers. Examples include an executor, administrator, trustee or guardian.

Corporation

A separate and distinct legal entity.

Corpus (body)

The capital or principal amount of an estate or trust.

Custodian

One whose duty it is to take care of something, such as an estate or property.

Decedent

A deceased individual.

Defined Contribution Plan

A retirement plan where the contribution amount is defined but the future benefit is based on the performance of the assets held within the plan.

Disclaimer

A repudiation of any interest in or claim to the subject of the action, such as rejection of any title, claim, interest, estate or trust.

Distribution

The dissemination of property to those entitled to receive it according to the terms of a will or trust agreement.

Domicile

The location of a person's permanent home; where they legally reside.

Donee

One who obtains a gift.

Donor

One who contributes a gift.

Duress

Unlawful constraint used to force a person to do some act against their will.

Enduring Power of Attorney

A legal document that allows an individual to designate another person to make legal decisions on the individual's behalf and continue to do so during the incompetency.

Estate

The total assets of a person at the time of their death.

Estate Plan

A plan for the administration and disposition of an individual's property during their lifetime and at their death; established in a will and one or more trust agreements.

Executor/Executrix

See *Last Will and Testament*.

Fair Market Value

The price at which a property is transferred between willing buyers and sellers who are both acting rationally and with complete knowledge of the situation.

Fiduciary

An individual or institution bearing a relationship of trust and responsibility for the benefit of another.

Gift Tax

This is a U.S. federal and state tax imposed on the transfer of property; to be paid by the donor rather than the recipient.

Grantor

This person grants property or property rights through a written instrument.

Gross Estate

The total value of an individual's property in an estate before liabilities are deducted.

Guardian

There is a legal relationship between a ward and a guardian. Wards are usually those who have been declared incompetent by the courts to make particular decisions on their own behalf. Court-appointed guardians act as surrogate decision-makers for the ward.

Guardian Ad Litem

A court-appointed person representing the interests of a minor or incompetent person in court and legal matters.

Guardian or Committee

A person legally appointed by a court to manage the affairs of an individual who may be physically or mentally incapacitated.

Heir

A person entitled by a will or by the court to inherit the estate of another.

Heirs-at-Law

The relatives of a person who has died without creating a valid will. These heirs inherit the property of the deceased.

Holographic Will

A handwritten will by the person making the will.

Incidents of Ownership

The rights the owner has under an insurance contract. Examples include the right to cash in the policy, to receive a loan on the value of the policy and to change the designated beneficiary.

Incompetent Person

A person who is legally not capable of managing their affairs because of a mental (not physical) handicap.

Inter Vivos Trust

A trust that is created during the settlor's lifetime.

Intestacy

When an individual dies without leaving a valid will.

Intestate

See *Last Will and Testament*.

Inventory

Refers to the list of items included in the estate of a deceased person.

Irrevocable Trust

See *Trusts*.

Joint and Survivorship

When a husband and wife are joint beneficiaries of an annuity. Upon the death of either, the remaining spouse becomes the sole beneficiary.

Joint Tenancy

Two or more people mutually holding legal title to property. In the event that one owner dies, the surviving owner receives the entire property.

Last Will

The last will a person completes. All former wills are invalid; this term is used to emphasize the fact that it is the most current and effective will of the maker.

Last Will and Testament

A will is perhaps the most well-known means of disposing of property at death. Every jurisdiction in Canada has its own rules for making a valid will, with each setting out requirements for a will to be valid in that jurisdiction. The person nominated by the testator to wind down the affairs of the decedent is called the personal representative (also known as executor or executrix). When a person with a will dies, they are said to die testate. This means that the will governs the disposition of that person's property. A person dying intestate has no valid last will and testament.

Letters of Administration

A legal document issued by a probate court that gives the administrator authority to take control of assets in the deceased person's name.

Letters Testamentary

A legal document by a court giving an executor power to take control of and distribute property.

Lien

A legal claim against a property; security for payment of an obligation.

Living Will

A directive to physicians in which an individual expresses their desire not to be kept alive by extraordinary means when they are determined to be in a terminal condition. This document directs the physician to give or withhold life sustaining medical care. The principal should state in the living will the conditions under which treatments should be continued or discontinued, and what types of life-sustaining efforts should be made.

Lump Sum Distribution

One lump sum payment of an individual's retirement plan benefits rather than equal payments over a specific period of time.

Minor

A person under legal age; meaning under the age where they are granted full legal rights. For tax purposes, a person who has not attained the age of 18 in the calendar year is a minor.

Notary Public

A person authorized by the province or territory to certify documents.

Notice to Creditors

A public notice to creditors of an estate to present their claims for what the executor or administrator owes them out of the estate.

Pension Plans (defined benefit plan)

A traditional retirement plan offered by some employers that pays a set amount each year during retirement. They are company pensions that guarantee a specific amount of benefits to employees.

Personal Representative

A person who manages the legal affairs of another, such as an executor or administrator.

Powers of Attorney

A document whereby one person (the "principal") authorizes someone else (the "agent" or the "attorney-in-fact") to act on their behalf. A power of attorney may be general, granting broad authority to make decisions concerning investments, tax matters and property transactions, or it may be specific, granting only limited authority to perform one or more specific duties. Every province and territory has legislation authorizing the creation and use of powers of attorney. In all cases, the principal must be competent when the power of attorney is executed. Note: there are different kinds of powers of attorney that are also called advance directives (see definition above).

Probate (verb)

A legal process where a deceased person's estate is administered and distributed; includes payment of outstanding obligations.

Probate Court

This court has jurisdiction over a deceased person's estate and also over people under guardianship.

Probate of Will

Presentation of proof before a court to establish the validity of a will and to admit a will to probate.

Profit-Sharing Plan

This plan provides employees with a share of the net profits of the business (in addition to their regular wages).

Qualified Domestic Relations Order (QDRO)

A court order accounting for the assignment of marital property, generally employee benefits, to an alternate payee such as a spouse or dependant.

Quick Claim Deed

Conveyance of real property.

Residue

The remaining portion of a deceased person's estate after all payments (debts, expenses, etc.) have been made.

Revocable Trust

See *Trusts*.

Revocation

The act of making a will or a trust instrument void.

Services for the Elderly Client

Services offered by CAs to design, implement and monitor financial strategies for maturing families and individuals to assist them in maintaining and enjoying their personal independence.

Simultaneous Death

When two or more people die and the order of their death cannot be determined.

Successor Trustee

When an original trustee dies or becomes incapable of managing their own trust, this person(s) becomes responsible for management of the trust.

Tenancy by the Entirety

Joint ownership of real property by a husband and wife in which both have rights to the property. Upon the death of either the other has the title through the right of survivorship.

Tenancy in Common

When two or more owners share a stated portion of property. Upon the death of one owner, their portion does not go to the remaining owner(s), but to the deceased owner's heirs.

Testamentary Capacity

The mental ability to comprehend how to make a valid will.

Testamentary Trust

A testamentary trust is usually created by the maker's will, funded by the estate and administered by a trustee named in the will.

Testate

See *Last Will and Testament.*

Testator

See *Last Will and Testament*.

Testatrix

See *Last Will and Testament*.

Trustee

A trustee manages the trust for the benefit of the trust beneficiaries. A trustee is required to meet a certain standard of care when administering their duties and powers, which are set out in the trust document and applicable trust legislation. Trustees are also required to meet the requirements of the applicable *Income Tax Act* provisions when administering a trust.

Trusts

Trusts are legal arrangements by which the legal ownership and the beneficial ownership of assets are separated. Trusts can be divided into two major categories—irrevocable or revocable. Irrevocable trusts cannot be changed (with very few exceptions) once they are put in place. Revocable trusts can be amended and/or changed.

Trust Company

A corporation engaging in the trust business; serves both individuals and business organizations.

Trust Instrument

A document that establishes a trust. Examples include a will, trust agreement, declaration of trust, deed of trust or order of court.

Trust under Will

See *Testamentary Trust*.

Vesting

When a person has received a benefit right, which is attributed to employer contributions, and is not contingent upon the person's duration of employment.

Ward

There is a legal relationship between a ward and a guardian. Wards are usually persons who have been declared incompetent by the courts to make particular decisions on their own behalf. Court-appointed guardians act as surrogate decision-makers for the ward.

Warranty Deed

A deed in which the seller guarantees the title is good; the deed contains covenants of title.

Will

A legal document stating a person's desires regarding how and to whom they want their property distributed after they die.